SEA DEFENCE AND
COAST PROTECTION WORKS

Da wearth micel styrung geworden on thaere sae . . .

Matthew 8:24

SEA DEFENCE AND COAST PROTECTION WORKS

A guide to design

Roland Berkeley Thorn
BSc, CEng, FICE, FIWES, MIStructE, MBIM
Consultant

Andrew G. Roberts
CEng, MIMunE,
Principal Engineer, Canterbury City Council

THOMAS TELFORD LTD
1981

Thomas Telford Ltd, Telford House, 26–34 Old Street, London EC1

© R. Berkeley Thorn and A. G. Roberts, 1981

ISBN 07277 0085 5

Publishing history
First published in 1960 by Butterworth & Co. (Publishers) Ltd under the
title *The Design of Sea Defence Works*
Second edition, *Sea Defence Works*, published in 1971
Third edition, which has been totally revised and updated, published in 1981
by Thomas Telford Ltd under the title *Sea Defence and Coast Protection Works*

Photoset in 11/12pt Baskerville, printed and bound in Great Britain by
Redwood Burn Ltd, Trowbridge, Wiltshire

We dedicate this book to

R. C. H. RUSSELL

and his staff at the Hydraulics Research Station, Wallingford

in recognition of the immense contribution their basic and *ad hoc* research work has made to our greater understanding of the many factors affecting the design of sea defence and coast protection works. In so doing, we recognise the outstanding contributions also made by the United States Army Coastal Engineering Research Center and by Dutch Engineers

Acknowledgements

The authors' thanks are due to the following. D. W. Briant, Southern Water Authority, for photographs, details and descriptions of Southern Water Authority sea defence works; G. Cole, Ministry of Agriculture, Fisheries and Food, for descriptions of and extracts from Flood Protection Research Committee Reports; L. Draper and M. Darbyshire, Institute of Oceanographic Sciences, for wave prediction curves; J. Evans, Consultant, for photograph of Pett Sea Wall; B. E. Hardy, Canterbury City Council, for photographs, details and descriptions of Canterbury City Council coast protection works; N. J. Heaf, Atkins Research and Development, for description of REFRAC Program; Institution of Civil Engineers, for Darbyshire and Draper wave prediction curves, extract from Paper by D. E. Newman and run-up curves from *Floods and Reservoir Safety*; R. E. L. Lelliott, Bournemouth Borough Council, for photograph of foreshore at Bournemouth; M. E. Pindard, Faber & Faber Ltd, for extract in Old English from *The Tree of Language* by H. and C. Laird; R. C. H. Russell, Hydraulics Research Station, and HMSO, for photographs of the Sheerness Sea Wall model and foreshore at Bournemouth; The Director of the Construction Industry Research and Information Association, for data from CIRIA Report 61; US Army Coastal Engineering Research Center, for SMB wave prediction curves; A. F. Whillock, Consultant, for photograph of W blocks.

The authors are deeply indebted to staff at the Hydraulics Research Station, the Institute of Oceanographic Sciences, the Ministry of Agriculture, Fisheries and Food, the Southern Water Authority, the Canterbury City Council and other organisations, who have provided source material and in many cases advice in the preparation of the text, particularly the following: N. W. A. Allsop; D. W. Briant; P. Brooks; L. Draper; J. Driver; L. J. Jaffrey; T. W. Kermode; I. H. Mackinder; L. M. Manley; L. H. Miller; G. M. Motyka; D. E. Newman; J. M. A. Pontin; R. D. Powell; W. A. Price; G. W. Roberts; J. E. Robson; E. C. Penning-Rowsell; P. J. Stevens; M. R. Watson; A. F. Whillock.

Sections 3.6, 3.7 and 3.8 were contributed by M. R. Watson, BSc (Eng), CEng, MICE (Balfour Beatty Construction Ltd).

Preface

Recent years have seen a great increase in the multidisciplinary services needed in the design of major sea defence and coast protection works, if full advantage is to be taken of the latest design methods and the use of computers.

The Meteorological Office has facilities for providing the probabilities of given wind strengths, directions and durations; the Institute of Oceanographic Sciences can provide deep water wave heights, periods associated with wind strengths, directions and durations, return periods of tide levels and rates of secular rise of sea level. Hydraulics laboratories such as the Hydraulics Research Station, Wallingford carry out physical and numerical (computer) model investigations, while soil mechanics laboratories are available for soil investigations with associated computer programs. Thus, even if it were practicable, a comprehensive book on the design of sea defence and coast protection works would be prohibitively expensive. This book, therefore, as its title makes clear, is a *guide*. It sets out the basics with sufficient information to enable outline solutions to be found for most problems and it lays stress upon the most recent design approaches available, in particular, the probabilistic method of design with the use of physical and numerical models with irregular waves. Of equal importance, it gives sufficient further information and references to enable the solutions to be worked out in full detail. ‾

Sea defence works protect low-lying land that would be flooded if the defences were breached, and are constructed and maintained by Water Authorities under the Water Act, 1973, and the Land Drainage Act, 1976. Coast protection works in essence are for the protection from erosion of higher land and are constructed and maintained by Coast Protection Authorities (Maritime District Councils), under the Coast Protection Act, 1949.

The need of the seaborne landings of the Second World War for wave information gave a stimulus to the study of coastal hydraulics. This continued in America in the activities of the Beach Erosion Board of the United States Army Corps of Engineers (now the US Army Coastal Engineering Research Center), and in the United Kingdom at the Hydraulics Research Station at Wallingford. Work was further encouraged by the setting up in Britain of the Advisory Committee on Sea Defence Research, now replaced by the Flood Protection Research Committee. Design has also greatly benefited from the many investigations in the last decade or so carried out for off-shore structures.

In *The Design of Sea Defence Works*, published by Butterworths in 1960, my aim was to deal with the subject in a way that was based soundly on experience and upon the principles and findings of coastal hydraulics. Ten years later, my colleague J. C. F. Simmons and I re-examined the text and revised and metricated it for a second edition, *Sea Defence Works*, published in 1971 by Butterworths, to whom I am most grateful for assigning to me the copyright of that edition.

Major advances since that date indicate the need for further review. For this reason the present volume has been written. Unlike the second edition, the present book is a major re-write incorporating the extensive relevant developments of recent years. Many problems are common to both sea defence and coast protection works. Some problems, however, are mainly related to coast protection, for example, cliff stabilisation, and therefore a separate chapter has been included dealing with these matters, written by my co-author, Andrew Roberts. However, his influence on the book has extended widely beyond that chapter, and I record my appreciation of the many suggestions he has made which have helped to shape its contents.

Under Acknowledgements we list those without whose help the book could not have been written. Our thanks are especially due to M. R. Watson, G. M. Motyka and L. Draper.

Little Rede   R. B. T.
Banky Meadow
Barming
Kent

Contents

Chapter 1

Tides and waves

1.1 TIDES GENERALLY

From the earliest times, in Europe, the relationship between the tides and the phases of the moon has been realised. It was known that the highest high water levels and the greatest difference in levels between high and low water (spring tide) occurred about two days after the times of full or new moon, approximately every 15 days, and that the lowest high water levels and the least difference in levels between high and low water (neap tide) also occurred every 15 days near the times of half moon at the first and last quarters.

1.2 TIDE TABLES

The sea defence engineer is mainly concerned with the results of tidal research and only very indirectly with the mathematical theory. A great deal of practical information will be found in the Admiralty Tide Tables.[1] The information given is:

(*a*) times and levels of high and low water on any day at standard and secondary ports round the coast
(*b*) mean high and low water spring tides, mean high and low water neap tides, mean tide level, at ports round the coast
(*c*) height of the tide at a given time, and time at which the tide reaches a given height at ports round the coast.

1.3 EFFECT ON TIDE LEVELS OF BAROMETRIC PRESSURE AND WIND

A change in atmospheric pressure of 25 mm Hg can cause a change of about 0.3 m in sea level. Sea levels are raised by

1

winds in the direction towards which the winds are blowing, and conversely are lowered in the direction from which the winds are coming. The converging or diverging of coastlines increases or decreases these variations in sea level. For example, water driven into or out of the more confined area of the southern part of the North Sea by northerly or southerly gales considerably affects sea levels in the Thames Estuary, producing material variations from the predicted tide levels. In the open sea, however, winds alone would not generally alter the level by more than about 0.3 m.

1.4 TIDAL STREAMS

With the flow and ebb of the tide are associated tidal streams along the coast. In shallow channels the tidal curve can become distorted, the rise becoming more rapid than the fall; under these conditions the tidal current is greater on the flood tide than on the ebb tide, which is in the opposite direction. All along the coast the inshore current need not necessarily be in the same direction as the offshore tidal stream. For example, the effect of a headland may be to cause an eddy giving an inshore current locally in the opposite direction to the tidal stream. Information with regard to the directions and velocities of tidal streams at definite points and at tabulated periods in hours before and after high water at a nearby port may be obtained from the relevant Admiralty Charts.

1.5 SURGES AND SEICHES

Large increases in sea level caused by the meteorological conditions described in Section 1.3 and of speed and direction similar to that of the tidal wave are known as storm surges. Fig. 1 shows the tide levels recorded on 31 Jan./1 Feb. 1953 at Southend and the surge that was superimposed on the tide. High water was nearly 2.5 m above the predicted level. A good account of surge mechanism is given by C. A. M. King in *Beaches and Coasts*.[2]

Seiches are also non-tidal fluctuations in sea level, but of short oscillation period compared with tidal waves and are caused by sudden meteorological conditions such as the

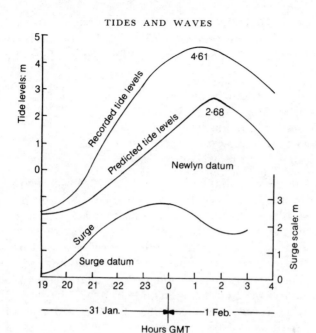

Fig. 1. Tide level curve at Southend on 31 Jan./1 Feb. 1953 (based on Port of London Authority data)

passage of a line squall. The seiche that occurred on 3 July 1946 on the south coast of England caused the sea level to drop 1.25 m in a few minutes and then to rise rapidly 2.5 m.

1.6 SECULAR RISE IN SEA LEVEL

For hundreds of years the south east of England has been sinking in relation to sea level, and the northern part of the British Isles has been rising, probably partly as a result of land tilt and partly as a result of the continued melting of the polar ice cap.

The study of secular variation in sea level caused by this and also affected by the local morphology and other causes at present not understood, requires a reliable series of annual mean sea level values calculated from an averaging of the observed hourly values. The data are further analysed in correlation with meteorological pressure time series applicable to the ports concerned and the period concerned.

3

In a study for the Southern Water Authority, the Institute of Oceanographic Sciences found the following values of annual secular rise:

Newlyn 1.95 mm/year
Southampton 1.06 mm/year
Newhaven 4.11 mm/year
Dover 4.52 mm/year
Southend 1.71 mm/year

It will be seen that these values differ from port to port. In determining the return periods of tide levels, it is important to take secular rise into account. This is dealt with in detail in Section 1.9. The Institute of Oceanographic Sciences study showed that generally the trends in mean sea level were very similar to the trends in annual sea level maxima (see Section 1.9). For further information on this matter, the reader is referred to work by Blackman and Graff.[3]

Further recent investigations[4,5] have shown that in some cases analysis of different portions of the data series can give results differing from the analysis of the full data. Where this is not the case, that is, where a mean trend is apparent throughout, as for example for south west England and south Wales, then the results based on the full (or even part) data may be used with confidence. However, where these variations exist, for example in south east and north west England, then for the purposes of design a judgement has to be made based on other considerations. This point is dealt with further in Section 1.9.

1.7 WAVES AND SWELL

When ideal waves move over deep water all water particles move in vertical circles, the diameter of the circles described by the surface particles being equal to the wave height H, that is the height in metres from crest to trough, and the diameters decreasing with depth. The movement decreases rapidly with depth, so that below a depth of one wave length the movement is less than 1/500 of the wave height. In shallow water, that is, when the depth is equal to or less than half the wave length, the water particle orbits become ellipses with their major axes horizontal. For intermediate depths, the orbits are circular

4

towards the surface and elliptical towards the bottom. With increasing depth the vertical motion diminishes more rapidly than the horizontal motion, so that the deeper the particle, the flatter its orbit.

Wind-generated waves, except in the form of ocean swell on calm water, cannot strictly be termed ideal, although for practical purposes they may be regarded as behaving very similarly. The characteristic shape of wind-driven waves is a steep slope on the leeward side of the crest and a gentler slope on the windward side. Ocean swell, which is wind-generated waves that are beyond the area in which they were generated, are much more regular.

Where a swell arrives in an area where waves are being generated by a local wind, the wave heights do not add linearly. The combined height may be taken approximately as the square root of the sum of the squares of the two wave heights.

1.8 MASS TRANSPORT AND RIP CURRENTS

The forward movement of the water particles is not entirely compensated for by backward movement and as a result there is a general movement of water in the direction of travel of the waves—this is known as mass transport or wave set-up. When waves reach the coast, therefore, the sea level rises and there is flow from regions of high waves to regions of low waves and to the sea. Narrow bands of water moving away from the shore are called rip currents and constitute a means whereby water brought to the coast by mass transport returns out to sea.

A strong wind can also increase water levels locally, the wind stresses on the surface raising the water to leewards, against a shore or in an estuary. This is called wind set-up.

1.9 RETURN PERIODS OF TIDE LEVELS

In 1963, Suthons and Lennon presented papers on abnormally high sea levels.[6,7] The statistical method of analysis of annual observed sea level maxima used by Suthons was that of Jenkinson,[8] known as the General Extreme Value Method, which depends on the assumption that a series of extreme events is random or contains a linear trend. Suthons found that for most of the south east ports there was a linear trend of about 3 mm per year. If a linear trend exists, the annual maxima are reduced to a standard date.

Suthons therefore produced port diagrams and tabulations giving, for each port, the return periods of given tide levels being equalled or exceeded, related to a given date. From these data the corresponding level for a given return period may be calculated for any other date, by adding or subtracting the estimated annual linear trend multiplied by the difference in years between the two dates.

In 1976, the Southern Water Authority asked the Institute of Oceanographic Sciences to carry out a similar study for ten ports on the south coast of England within their area, including those previously studied by Suthons. Jenkinson's method was programmed for computer and the series of annual maxima for each port were analysed.

The study showed differing linear trends from port to port (see Section 1.6). To investigate this further, the series of annual mean sea level for six of the ports were analysed, and generally the trends in mean sea level were found to be in close agreement with the trends in annual maxima.

The Institute of Oceanographic Sciences study produced a report[9] providing port diagrams giving return periods of given tide levels being equalled or exceeded related to the year 1976.

Generally, therefore, provided there are sufficient reliable tide level data, it is possible by this method to provide return periods of given tide levels related to given lengths of coast. As there are some differences between the definitions given by the authors referred to in this section for the term 'return period', for a rigorous interpretation and application of their results, each author's definition should be carefully studied.

However, where secular rise is taken into account, the above approach is based on mean linear trends derived from the full data. But recent investigations (see Section 1.6) show that in some cases analysis of different portions of the data series can give results differing from those obtained from the full data. In such cases, for the purposes of design, judgements have to be made based on other considerations. For example, if a nuclear power station were being protected, it might be prudent from an examination of the results of the analyses to base the design on the results that lead to the highest tide levels in relation to return periods.

An alternative method was used for Maplin by Ackers and Ruxton.[10] The frequencies of high water surge residuals (obtained by subtracting predicted astronomical tides from observed tide levels) were calculated. The frequencies of predicted tides over a five year period were also studied. The combined frequency of statistically independent events is the product of their separate frequencies. Hence the combined frequencies of predicted tides and surges were obtained and provided a synthesised record of extreme water levels extending to events with a return period of 1000 years, without extrapolating beyond the range of observed surge residuals and predicted tides.

There is implicit in this approach the assumption that the probability distribution of surges is the same for all predicted tide levels. However, in shallow water, a tide–surge interaction can occur, that is, tides and surges are not independent. This difficulty can be overcome by determining separate surge probabilities related to different parts of the tidal range (see references 11 and 12).

While extreme tide levels are usually stated in terms of return periods, for obtaining the return periods of combined tide levels and wave heights (see Section 1.16), it is more convenient to have the tide level information in the form of probabilities rather than return periods. If r is the return period in years, i the interval between occurrences in years and p the probability, then $r = i/p$. Since there are 705 high waters per annum, $i = 1/705$, hence with this value of i, and a known value of r, p is found. The probability of the tide level being in a given incremental range is the difference between the probabilities of the upper and lower values of the range.

Lennon[7] put forward tentatively an expression for given lengths of coast relating given extreme tide levels to mean high water spring (MHWS) tide levels and spring tide range, that is, regional dimensionless factors equal to

$$\frac{T_e - \text{MHWS}}{\text{MHWS} - \text{MLWS}}$$

7

Table 1.1. Wind strength

Force (Beaufort Scale)	Sea miles, 6080 ft/h	km/h	Wind
0	0–1	0–2	
1–2	2–6	4–11	
3	7–10	13–18	light
4	11–16	20–30	moderate
5	17–21	32–39	moderate
6	22–27	41–50	strong
7	28–33	52–61	strong
8	34–40	63–74	gale
9	41–47	76–87	gale
10	48–55	89–102	storm
11	56–65	104–120	storm
12	over 65	120	hurricane

where T_e is the extreme tide level, and MLWS is mean low water spring tide level.

Values of this factor, for example for the 50 year return period tide level, are Dover 0.22, Sheerness 0.26, Southend 0.26.

Hence, if for a length of coast along which the value of this factor for a given return period is approximately constant, the standard tide data at points along it are known and the extreme tide level corresponding to the given return period at one point is also known, then the tide level corresponding to the same return period at the other points can be calculated.

Further investigation of regional factors is desirable and until this has been done, the foregoing expression should be used with caution. Present indications are that this approach might not always be closely applicable to confined waters, as for example, the eastern end of the English Channel, or in the vicinities of estuaries.

1.10   WIND FORCE

Wind force and direction are of importance to sea defence engineers and in meteorological reports the strength of the wind is usually given in accordance with the Beaufort Scale (Table 1.1).

1.11   REGULAR AND IRREGULAR WAVES

For regular (uniform) waves the wave period P is the time in seconds between the passing of two adjacent crests past a stationary point. The wave length L is the distance in metres between two adjacent crests, and if V is the velocity in metres per second of the wave, $L = PV$.

Airy's expression for the velocity of individual waves, the phase velocity, is

$$V = \sqrt{\left(\frac{gL}{2\pi} \tanh \frac{2\pi D}{L} \right)}$$

where D is the still water depth in metres and g is the acceleration due to the force of gravity. When D becomes greater than L, $\tanh 2\pi D/L$ becomes equal to unity, so that in deep water

$$V = \sqrt{\left(\frac{gL}{2\pi} \right)} = 1.25 \sqrt{L}$$

The velocity of a group of waves, the group velocity, is not necessarily the same as that of individual waves in the group. It can be shown (reference 13, section 2.237, velocity of a wave group) that in a wave group comprising two sinusoidal wave trains of slightly different wave length and period but of the same wave height, in deep water the group velocity V_g is half the phase velocity V, whereas in shallow water the group and phase velocities are the same, the connecting expression being

$$V_g/V = \tfrac{1}{2} \left[1 + \frac{4\pi D/L}{\sinh (4\pi D/L)} \right]$$

When the depth becomes less than one tenth of the wave length, $\tanh 2\pi D/L$ approaches $2\pi D/L$ and V then equals $\sqrt{gD}$. This is the expression often of most use to sea defence engineers. It has been found that generally these expressions can be applied with only a small error to natural wind-generated waves and therefore their use in sea defence design problems is considerable. Wave velocities for various depths may be read directly from Design Chart A.

The kinetic and potential components of wave energy are equal and the total wave energy in one wave length per unit crest width is $wH^2L/8$ or $\rho g H^2L/8$, where w is the unit weight of

9

sea water and $\rho = w/g$. The total average wave energy per unit of surface area is therefore $\rho g H^2/8$, which is known as the energy density or specific energy.

The wave energy that is transmitted forward, neglecting bottom friction, remains nearly constant as the wave moves inshore. This principle, that the wave energy remains constant between adjoining orthogonals, is the basis of determining the change in wave height caused by refraction (see Section 1.12). Group velocity is important because it can be shown that the rate at which energy is transmitted forward per unit wave-crest width (wave energy flux) is equal to the group velocity times the energy density.

For irregular waves, the wave period P_r, called the zero crossing wave period, is the time between two successive down-crossings of the mean water level by the water surface. The mean zero crossing period $\bar{P}_r$, is the average of the P_r values; P_s is the significant wave period, that is, the mean period of the waves associated with the highest third of the waves, and $\bar{P}_r$ can be taken as equal to $0.91P_s$ (see reference 14). In the English Channel, the wave period does not usually exceed 6 s and commonly for waves in the Atlantic it is from 6 to 8 s.

The significant wave height $\bar{H}_s$ is defined as the average height of the highest one third of the waves (for the relationship between maximum wave height and significant wave height, see Section 1.14). More rigorously, the significant height $\bar{H}_s$ is used, the average height of the highest one third of the waves defined by zero down-crossings of the mean water level by the water surface. The wave frequency f is the reciprocal of the period, in hertz (1 hertz is 1 cycle per second).

In steady wind conditions, irregular waves vary in height and period according to probability distributions[15] which are characterised by and can be obtained from the wave spectrum which is related to $\bar{H}_s$ and $\bar{P}_r$ (and hence f).

Irregular waves can be taken as a combination of sine waves of different heights and frequencies randomly phased to each other. This leads to the wave spectrum (also known as the energy spectrum, or energy density spectrum), which is a plot of energy density in units of (metres)^2 per frequency against wave frequency in units of cycles per second. It gives the quantity of energy related to each of the different frequencies. The ordinates of the spectrum represent wave height squared per frequency. The area of the spectrum has therefore the dimensions of (metres)^2. It can be demonstrated from empirical data that $\bar{H}_s = 4$ (area under the curve)$^{1/2}$.

The use of wave spectra in simulating the effects of irregular waves in models is dealt with in Section 4.8, which also draws attention to the need in some cases to take also into account the occurrence and frequency of characteristic wave patterns.

When the depth of the water becomes less than half the wave length, not only do the velocity and length of the waves decrease, but the height also alters. The expression for determining this effect, assuming bottom friction effects are negligible, is given in Section 1.12. There is also the effect of bottom friction and this is referred to in Section 1.13 (see also reference 16).

As the bed continues to rise, the wave eventually breaks. There are four main modes in which waves break, depending on the value of the Battjes function $\tan \beta / \sqrt{(2\pi H_o/gP^2)}$, where β is the bed slope and H_o the deep sea wave height. The names of these modes are self-explanatory. On very flat slopes the wave breaks by spilling; on steeper slopes, by plunging; on very steep slopes, generally steeper than 2:1, by surging, that is, an action similar to a clapotis (see Section 1.17). There is a fourth mode intermediate between plunging and surging, called collapsing. Typical values of the Battjes function, the surf similarity parameter, given by Battjes are: spilling, 0.2; plunging, 0.5, 1.5; collapsing, 3; surging, 5 (see also Section 1.17).

The depth in which the wave breaks D_b, is very approximately equal to 1.28 times the breaking wave height H_b, which in turn, on a steep apron can approach twice the deep sea wave height. For a plunging wave, as much as 78% of it at breaking can be above still water level but it could also be 50% or less. In fact D_b/H_b varies with the slope of the foreshore and the steepness of the wave. The steeper the wave and the steeper the bed, the greater the breaking depth. Hence the relationship $D_b = 1.28H_b$ is only approximate. For a more precise assessment, taking these factors into account see reference 17. D_b is related to the deep sea wave height, H_o, by $H_o = 2.23D_b (H_o/P^2)^{1/3}$ in metric units. Figs. 2, 3, 4 and 5, illustrate typically the way a wave breaks on a sloping sea wall apron.

Fig. 2. Wave breaking on a sloping sea wall apron

Fig. 3. Wave breaking on a sloping sea wall apron

Fig. 4.   Wave breaking on a sloping sea wall apron

Fig. 5.   Wave breaking on a sloping sea wall apron

13

1.12 WAVE REFRACTION AND DIFFRACTION

As waves approach a shore obliquely and the depth becomes less than half the deep sea wave length, the portions of the wave nearest the shore slow down so that the wave crests swing round and tend to become parallel to the shore—this is called refraction. In refraction, as in reflection, sea waves behave similarly to light waves. It is thus possible, by constructing one or more raised areas on the sea bed, to deviate waves passing over them, so that calm water occurs at harbour entrances while on either side of the entrances heavy wave action continues. Refraction may have a divergent or convergent effect on the waves, the wave heights being decreased or increased respectively. Refraction can obviously also be caused by currents causing differences in actual speeds of waves.

The effects of refraction can be determined graphically and the method is set out in detail in reference 13, Section 2.3 (see also reference 18). The basis of the method, which assumes that the wave energy between adjoining orthogonals remains constant (neglecting bottom friction), is first to plot underwater contours for various depth intervals. Next, perpendicular to the deep water crest line, orthogonals are drawn. The change in direction of an orthogonal as it passes over a bottom contour is

$$\sin a_2 = (V_2/V_1) \sin a_1$$

where a_1 is the angle the wave crest makes with the underwater contour over which it is passing, a_2 is the angle the wave crest makes as it passes over the next underwater contour, V_1 is the wave (phase) velocity at the first underwater contour and V_2 is the wave (phase) velocity at the second underwater contour. Thus, the change in direction of the orthogonals is found and hence the wave refraction pattern is plotted.

To carry out the technique of graphical analysis of wave refraction a chart of the area under study must be obtained. This chart should show water depth and should extend offshore to a distance where the water depth is equal to half the longest wave length under consideration. This chart is first contoured by joining the points of equal level. Once this is completed an assessment is made of the mid-contour position, this

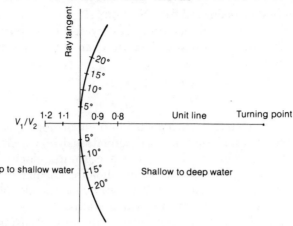

Fig. 6. Ray plotter

being the average position between successive contours, and this mid-contour is marked on the chart. The technique of wave refraction described here should be applied to a number of different orthogonal approach angles.

By reference to Fig. 6, a ray plotter should be constructed on a transparent film or paper overlay to a suitable size. Then, using the formula just given, the ratios of velocities can be calculated. Values of V_1/V_2 will be greater than unity for a decreasing water depth condition and less than unity for an increasing water depth condition. Such a calculated ratio should be noted.

At the point where the orthogonal cuts the mid-contour a perpendicular line to the orthogonal is constructed. The ray plotter is then overlaid in such a way as to establish a turning point along the perpendicular. Using this point the ray tangent is rotated until the value of the ratio of velocity change, previously calculated and identified on the ray plotter, cuts the same mid-contour. A new orthogonal may then be struck using the tangent on the ray plotter. This process is repeated for successive mid-contours. Such a technique is recommended for its simplicity and ease of use, and although requiring time to execute provides valuable guidance to the designer. However, generally the computer techniques described here are as easy and more sophisticated in their result.

It will have been seen from Section 1.11 that the wave energy transmitted forward per unit crest width is proportional to $H^2 V_g$. It follows therefore that the change in wave height is given by

$$\frac{H_1}{H_o} = \left(\frac{V_{og} b_o}{V_g b}\right)^{1/2}$$

where b is the distance between adjoining orthogonals; b_o is the distance between adjoining orthogonals in deep water; V_g is the wave group velocity; V_{og} is the wave group velocity in deep water. Here V_{og}/V_g is known as the shoaling coefficient and b_o/b as the refraction coefficient. The *Shore Protection Manual*[13] provides Tables to facilitate these calculations.

For a more advanced treatment of the subject, using irregular waves, known as the spectrum refraction method, see references 19 and 20.

Diffraction occurs when energy is transferred along a wave crest and results from the effects on the waves of obstructions such as harbour arms or headlands. It is of importance in the design of harbours, but generally of less importance in the design of sea defence works, since the more critical conditions for the design of sea defence works are usually those arising from directions from which the headland gives no shelter.

The *Shore Protection Manual*,[13] gives in Section 2.42 diagrams for determining diffraction based on Wiegel's method. This section also deals with diffraction of waves passing through gaps and also the problem of combined refraction and diffraction. On the subject of diffraction the reader is also referred to references 18 and 19.

1.13   NUMERICAL MODELS FOR REFRACTION

It will be seen in Section 1.15 that modern design methods require the inshore wave heights to be determined from the deep sea wave heights. The Hydraulics Research Station has, as an alternative to the graphical method, a numerical model that does this, taking into account refraction, shoaling and bed friction (see references 19 and 20).

Other sources also have computer programs available, for example the Atkins Franlab Marine Ltd, Epsom, REFRAC

16

program, which also takes into account refraction, shoaling and bottom friction.

Two types of output are available for each run of their program. The primary output is on a computer-controlled graph plotter, which is similar to a manually drawn refraction diagram. This shows wave orthogonals over the area under investigation and gives a direct indication of the wave direction. The relative wave height, calculated by the program, is plotted along each orthogonal at equal increments of time. This allows the height nodes to be joined easily by hand to show the successive wave-crest positions. The graphical output may be plotted to any scale, subject only to the limitations on paper size, and this allows the refraction diagrams to be overlaid directly on to charts or plans of the area. To facilitate orientation, the program may be instructed to draw a coastline or contours of the area and to mark the limits of the topographical data grid.

In addition to the graphical output, a tabulated set of results for each orthogonal is available from the line printer, and further details may be obtained from the firm as to the full extent of information that can be obtained from the program.

1.14 WIND GENERATED WAVE HEIGHT AND PERIOD IN DEEP AND SHALLOW WATER

As early as 1874 Thomas Stevenson put forward an expression which gives wave height in metres generated by gales. This is $H = 0.336\sqrt{F}$ (or $0.336\sqrt{F} + 0.762 - 0.261 \sqrt[4]{F}$ for fetches under 37 km), where F is the fetch in kilometres.

Although the expression does not take into account the actual wind strength, it has been found reliable in conditions where the wind duration has been sufficiently long. It is based upon data for the British Isles and may be taken to give the significant wave height.

Another approach which gives the wave heights and periods to be expected for given fetches and wind speeds, is that of Sverdrup, Munk and Bretschneider, the SMB method,[22] based on deep water wave data. The late Professor Francis of London University has shown that Stevenson's equations predict about the same wave height as the SMB method if the wind

17

speed is about 40 knots (74 km/h), that is for gale force winds (Beaufort 8–9) to which Stevenson intended his expressions to apply.

The SMB method gives the significant wave height, the significant wave period (and the wind duration necessary) to be expected for various fetches and various wind strengths.[22] Design Chart B is the SMB deep water prediction chart. Design Chart C gives direct readings of this information for gale force winds.

If the fetch width is less than 1.8 times the fetch length, the wave height is reduced. Thorndike Saville's method (reference 13, Section 3.432) for dealing with this, is, for wave height and wave period, to use an effective fetch. The ratios of effective fetch to actual fetch vary as follows for the fetch width/fetch length ratios: $W/F = 1.8$, $F_e/F = 1$; $W/F = 1$, $F_e/F = 0.9$; $W/F = 0.5$, $F_e/F = 0.67$; $W/F = 0.25$, $F_e/F = 0.46$.

In shallow water, for the same wind strengths and fetches, wave heights will be less than in deep water because of bed friction effects. The *Shore Protection Manual*[13] gives graphs for forecasting wave heights in shallow water for fetches up to 30 km and depths up to 15 m (see reference 13, Section 3.6). Design Charts D, E, F, G and H are plots of wave heights against fetches for gale force winds (Beaufort 8–9, 74 km/h) for various water depths.

From extensive data from a weather ship and from light ships around the coasts of Britain, Darbyshire and Draper[23] have produced graphs similar to the SMB graphs, but of particular application to the North Atlantic Ocean and British coastal waters and to similar areas. There are two sets of graphs, one for oceanic waters with a depth greater than 600 ft (183 m), and another for coastal waters with a mean depth of 100 ft (30 m) to 150 ft (46 m).

These graphs are reproduced (in metric form) in Charts I, J, K and L. To read for example Chart I, enter on the y axis at the point corresponding to the wind speed, follow this horizontally until it meets either the duration limit line or the fetch limit line, stopping at whichever is reached first, and then read off the wave height.

The figures obtained are the maximum wave height H_m and the significant period which would appear on a typical wave

18

record of 10 minutes duration containing about 100 waves. For practical purposes H_m may be taken to be equal to $1.6H_s$.

More recent work, for deep water (depth greater than a quarter of the longest wavelength in this context) is that of JONSWAP (Joint North Sea Wave Project).[24] This gives, in metric units, significant wave height as $16 \times 10^{-4} (FU^2/g)^{1/2}$ and the mean zero crossing period as $0.85/f_m$, where f_m is the frequency of the peak of the wave energy spectrum and is equal to $2.84g^{0.7}/(U^{0.4}F^{0.3})$; U is the surface wind speed at the 10 m elevation in metres per second; F is the fetch in metres and g the acceleration due to gravity in metres per second[2].

All these methods are based on data with considerable scatter. The best advice is to use the method based upon data derived from conditions which most closely resemble the conditions under consideration. For example, for the east coast of England, use the Darbyshire and Draper method, whereas for a fetch across a shallow estuary, the *Shore Protection Manual*[13] shallow depth predictions might be more suitable. Additionally, assistance can be obtained from the Institute of Oceanographic Sciences (a world wave data centre) using their (computer program based) method for predicting deep sea wave heights and periods.

For the north part of the North Sea, the Hydraulics Research Station NORSWAM program is also now available.[25] This is a numerical wave model to provide hindcast wave data for selected severe storms in the North Sea. The Meteorological Office also have a numerical wave forecasting model, which from the known conditions and the forecast windfield, predicts open sea waves in the vicinity of the United Kingdom up to 36 hours ahead.

Fortunately for the sea defence engineer, depth of water seaward of the wall is often a more important factor than fetch. In many cases it will be found that waves generated by the wind and fetch break and reform on sub-aqueous sandbanks or in the shallow water seaward of the wall, so that the height of the waves that break on the wall is determined by the depths of water seaward of the wall, for the waves break when the depth is roughly four thirds the breaking wave height. The relevant expressions connecting the breaking depth, the breaking wave height and the deep sea wave height are given in Section 1.11.

19

1.15   RETURN PERIODS OF WAVE HEIGHTS

There are a number of approaches to this problem. One is to divide into convenient sectors the directions from which waves can approach the length of coast being considered, then to work out the fetches for each of these sectors and the order of duration of blow for full wave height corresponding to the fetch (see Section 1.14), for wind strength ranges as appropriate, say, Beaufort 5–6, 7–8 and so on.

The probabilities of these wind strength ranges in these sectors with at least these durations of blow should, for most locations in the UK be obtainable from the Meteorological Office. If these wind durations are more than a few hours, it would be advisable to use instead the synthesised extended data method described further on.

Next, for each sector and each wind strength range, the corresponding wave height can be obtained from the Institute of Oceanographic Sciences or by the methods detailed in Section 1.14. The probabilities of the wind strength ranges and hence the probabilities of the corresponding wave heights (corrected, if necessary, for refraction and shallow water effects appropriate to the range of high water levels being considered) in each sector are thus obtained and from these by summation the probabilities of given wave height ranges are obtained for the length of coast being examined. The advantages of obtaining the answer in terms of probabilities of given wave height ranges will be seen in Sections 1.16 and 4.7.

For estimating the return periods of combined wave heights and tide levels (see Section 1.16), it is also necessary to ascertain from the Meteorological Office the average annual number of occasions on which these specified wind conditions occur.

An alternative approach is possible where the fetches are roughly similar and where there are nearby a light-ship, where wave heights can be recorded (usually short term), and a land station having long term records of wind strengths and directions. In these circumstances it is possible to obtain an empirical relationship between wave heights, for example, maximum daily significant wave height and on-shore maximum hourly mean wind speed (or other more suitable period corresponding to the fetch if the data are available or are estimated). Hence from the wind records it is possible to obtain the deep sea wave height probabilities. The wave heights can be corrected for refraction and shallow water effects appropriate to the range of high water levels being considered, to obtain the inshore wave heights. If the wave heights are to be put into given wave height incremental ranges (as required in Sections 1.16 and 4.7), for each incremental range the probability is the difference between the probabilities of the upper and lower figures of the range being equalled or exceeded.

On the matter of duration of blow, hourly mean wind speeds can be converted to longer duration means, by average factors determined by the Meteorological Office.[26]

If time is available, another method is to install a near shore wave recorder and relate the wave data from it to the onshore wind strengths and probabilities at the nearest anemometer station. This has the advantage that refraction corrections do not have to be made.

Of course, if wave records have been maintained over a sufficient number of years (or can be synthesised, see Section 1.14), the wave height probabilities can be obtained directly from the wave height data.

Literature on this subject is sparse, but see references 27 and 28.

1.16 RETURN PERIODS OF COMBINED WAVE HEIGHTS AND TIDE LEVELS

The probability of given inshore wave heights occurring is dealt with in Section 1.15 and that of given tide levels occurring in Section 1.9. If the two events are statistically independent, then their joint probability is the product of their separate probabilities. There is in this implicit the assumption that the wave height will be maintained long enough to coincide with high water. If sufficient concurrent wind and tide data are available, this assumption can be avoided by using for the wind/wave probability calculations data occurring with high tides (see reference 29).

A convenient joint probability matrix for this is set out in Table 1.2, based on Hydraulics Research Station usage.

21

Table 1.2. Joint probability matrix

Wave height (m)		Wave range probability	Tide level (m)	
Range	Central value		Range 6.75–7.25 Central value 7 (Range probability 0.1)	Range 7.25–7.75 Central value 7.5 (Range probability 0.2)
1.75–2.25	2.0	1.5×10^{-2}	1.5×10^{-3}	3×10^{-3}
2.25–2.75	2.5	1.0×10^{-2}	1.0×10^{-3}	2×10^{-3}

Hence it can be seen that the probability of the combination of the wave height range with central value 2.5 m with the tide level range with central value 7 m is 1.0×10^{-3}.

We are only concerned here with the specified wave heights occurring with high tides. If it is assumed that a high tide will always occur when one of the specified wave heights occurs, then, if the average annual number of occasions on which the tabulated waves occur (corresponding to their associated wind strengths) is 30, then the corresponding return period in years of this particular combination of wave height and tide level range is given by $r = i/p$, where i is the interval in years between joint occurrences of waves and tides, in this case 1/30, and p is the combined probability, in this case 1.0×10^{-3}, whence $r = 33.3$ years.

If there is perfect correlation, then the two events occur together, so that for this relationship, one simply tabulates together wave heights and tide levels that separately have the same probabilities.

However, in practice it is more likely that there could be a degree of correlation but not perfect correlation. Ackers and Ruxton, in their Maplin study,[10] in order to allow for the correlation between the incidence of surges and particular weather systems in the southern North Sea, classified the wind data into three populations, depending on whether there was a surge residual greater than 1m, less than 1m but greater than 0.6 m, and under 0.6 m, at high water on the day in question. The likelihood of winds and hence waves occurring with high water was then assessed by combining the chance of the two eventualities, wind frequency having been separated into these three surge associated populations. From a strictly statistical viewpoint, this approach is one of a series of conditional probabilities. It can happen, as in a case known to the Authors, that records show that the higher surges (most likely to affect design conditions) occur with winds in a given sector with a given fetch and this facilitates and makes more accurate the assessment of wave heights.

An example of the difference between the two extremes is provided by the Hydraulics Research Station's sea wall design study[27] for a section of the North Wales coast road, A55, at Llanddulas. The basis of the design was that specified overtopping discharges should occur only at specified long return periods. The discharge probabilities were computed twice, on the extreme assumptions of perfect correlation and perfect independence of the two events, wave heights and tide levels. For the same specified overtopping discharge and the same specified return period, the difference in height of the sea wall needed to be about 2 m between these two extremes. (A similar difference was also found in their Fleetwood Sea Wall investigations.[30]) For design purposes the perfect independence assumption was taken at Llanddulas which gives the lower wall height, since for this particular site, the indications were that the wave heights and tide levels were not strongly correlated. This aspect of part correlation between tides and waves is dealt with further in Section 4.7.

Another way of arriving at the return periods of combined wave heights and tide levels, is to tabulate down the left-hand side of the Table tide levels decreasing by equal increments and against them to enter the number of times, x, that those levels will be equalled or exceeded in 1000 years.

Horizontally along the top of the Table, enter onshore wind strengths increasing by equal increments and for each give the number of times y in a thousand that the wind strength will be equalled or exceeded (based on the probability of that onshore wind strength being equalled or exceeded on any day). It will be seen that the winds tabulated are onshore winds; that is the 'non-joint event' winds from other directions are thereby excluded.

23

Then, assuming the two events are independent, in the vertical columns under these wind strengths and on each horizontal line representing a tide level, write the product of x and y, which then represents the number of times in a million years that each particular combination of tide level and wind strength is likely to be equalled or exceeded and from which the return period of the combination can be obtained. Finally (as explained in Section 1.15) the return period values for the tide level/wind strength combinations are related to the corresponding tide level/wave height combinations. It will be seen in Section 4.7 that the method just described is not a convenient form for determining the return period of given overtopping being equalled or exceeded.

A third form of tabulation which (like the first form) is suitable for this purpose is to tabulate down the left-hand side of the Table tide levels decreasing by equal increments, and against each to enter the probability of that level being equalled or exceeded. Horizontally, along the top of the Table, from left to right, enter wave height ranges, say 3.5–4 m, 3–3.5 m and so on, and for each range, given the range probability. Then in each vertical column and on each horizontal line, enter the product of the tide probability and the wave height range probability, that is, the combined probability in each case of the tide level being equalled or exceeded with the wave height within the corresponding wave height range.

The Authors were first introduced to the second and third methods of tabulating given above by Binnie & Partners, Consultants.

Reference has been made in this Section to the assumptions of perfect independence, perfect correlation and part correlation. It can happen that for some coasts, high surge tides and high wave heights might be largely exclusive, in which case the assumption of independence would result in over-design.

For a more detailed account of the theory set out in this section, the reader is referred to references 27, 28, 31 and 32.

1.17 WAVE REFLECTION, CLAPOTIS AND SWASH

Waves approaching a vertical face (for example, a harbour arm) in sufficiently deep water (depth at least $1.5H$) and at an angle are reflected with the angle of incidence equal to the angle of reflection.

Under the same conditions, if the wave crests are parallel to the wall, the effect of reflection is to form a series of standing waves or clapotis. At fixed distances from the wall are nodes and anti-nodes; at the nodes there is no movement and at the anti-nodes there is maximum vertical movement from crest to trough. The wall is an anti-nodic position and the movement there from crest to trough is approximately twice the incident wave height. The effect of oblique incidence is to cause high crests to occur at the intersection of incident and reflected wave crests and low troughs to occur at the intersection of incident and reflected wave troughs. A wall slope of 2 : 1 (horizontal : vertical) is about the steepest for waves to break on it; if the apron is steeper, the wave is reflected and does not break. More exactly, Hunt has shown that the waves break on the slope when H_0/L_0 is greater than $0.19 \tan^2\alpha$, when α is the slope, H_0 the deep water wave height and L_0 the deep water wave length.

When a wave breaks on a foreshore or sea wall, the uprush of water is called the swash or run-up and the height to which it rises vertically above sea level is known as the swash height. This determines the height of shingle crests (the shingle full) and whether or not sea walls are overtopped. The more impermeable and steep the slope, the higher the swash height.

1.18   SWASH HEIGHTS AND OVERTOPPING

For a fully developed sea, Battjes gives the following expression for the swash height in metres vertically above still water level for a breaking wave (see Section 1.17) on simple slopes

$$z = 0.6\bar{P}_r\,(g\bar{H}_s)^{1/2}\tan\alpha$$

where z is the height exceeded by 2% of the run-up, $\bar{P}_r$ is the mean zero crossing period, g is the gravitational acceleration, $\bar{H}_s$ is the deep sea significant wave height, and α is the angle of the slope to the horizontal. The Dutch it seems use this 2% and also 2×10^{-3} m^3/s per metre as general rules for maximum permissible overtopping for unprotected landward slopes. Japanese studies suggest the following maxima, in m^3/s per metre, for the following, immediately behind the wall: man, 3×10^{-5}; car at low speed, 2×10^{-5}; house, damage limited to windows, 3×10^{-5}. For 10 m behind the crest, these rates can be increased tenfold (see reference 33). For a sea in the early stages of its growth, the coefficient 0.6 should be replaced by 0.75, which gives a greater run-up.

Battjes' work,[34,35] published in 1970/71 supersedes earlier Dutch and American work on simple slopes and, unlike previous American work, which only dealt with regular waves, provides for random waves.

For composite slopes, including those with berms, the Thorndike Saville method is available (Shore Protection Manual,[13] 7.2, Wave Run-up). This is based on regular waves and on replacing the composite slope by an equivalent simple slope intersecting the actual slope at the point where the wave breaks. Comparison of predicted values using this method with model experimental values showed the deviation generally within 10% with a maximum of about 25%. Work by Herbich and Sorensen indicated that the method should preferably be limited to cases where the berm width is less than 0.15 of the wave length. The Shore Protection Manual[13] presentation is extended to cover the run-up distribution of irregular waves by further publications by the US Army Coastal Engineering Center.[36,37]

The Hydraulics Research Station has produced a valuable publication[38] which extends Thorndike Saville's and Battjes' work to random waves on composite and bermed slopes. The publication sets out methods for determining the run-up with irregular waves on (a) composite slopes where the slope changes at the water level and (b) bermed slopes with equal slopes above and below a berm at water level. It includes graphs to facilitate the solutions. It is considered that the predicted run-up levels are accurate to within ± 10%. It should be noted that these graphs only apply to those cases where the water level coincides with either the point of change in slope or the berm level. The Thorndike Saville method is not subject to these limitations.

The methods discussed so far are for smooth, impermeable slopes. Swash heights on rough and permeable slopes are dealt with in reference 39. The corrections for swash height on shingle, depending on the size of the shingle, could be of the

26

order of a half for permeability and a fifth for roughness. See also references 36 and 37.

As has been seen, Battjes' expression is for the run up exceeded by 2% of the waves, a very small proportion. For initial studies Chart M may be used. This is from the Institution of Civil Engineers publication, *Flood and Reservoir Safety*. It gives values of z/H for various slopes, smooth faced, of rough stone, of shallow rubble, or of thick permeable riprap. The swash heights so given are based on an assumed wave steepness H/L of 0.05. If H is taken as the significant wave height, then the swash height is that reached or exceeded by 13% of the waves. If H is taken as 1.3 times the significant wave height, then the swash height is that reached or exceeded by 4% of the waves. (Hence, in the latter case, if the top of the wall were at swash height, fewer than one in twenty waves would cause overtopping.) Conversely, if the difference in levels between the water level and the top of the wall is known and taken as the swash height, the corresponding wave height may be deduced and the ratio of this to the significant wave height will indicate the percentage of the waves that will overtop the wall.

The smooth slope curve is based on that of Thorndike Saville.[40] The rough stone and the permeable riprap curves are based on the recommendations of the Technical Advisory Commission on Protection against Inundation.[41]

In most cases it is impracticable to construct walls up to swash height and some overtopping has to be accepted at the top of the tide under the designed conditions. A method of calculating the rate of overtopping where the crest of the wall is below swash height has been developed by Thorndike Saville (Shore Protection Manual,[13] 7.22, Wave Overtopping) for regular waves, and Ahrens and Titus[42] for irregular wave overtopping. These are useful for preliminary assessments. For more accurate determination of overtopping, model tests using random waves are needed. In this connection it should be borne in mind that random waves can give very much greater overtopping than that given by regular waves of height equal to the significant wave height of the random waves. Also, there can sometimes possibly be greater overtopping if, as usually happens, the waves are oblique to the wall. It is not possible to generalise on this. For example, model tests on the Queenbo-

27

rough Wall (Fig. 60) showed that when the angle of incidence was increased from 0° to 45° there was a considerable *decrease* in overtopping. In another case, it is understood that maximum overtopping occurred with an angle of incidence of about 15°.

1.19 WAVE PRESSURE ON VERTICAL WALLS

When waves are reflected and do not break, a matter mainly the concern of the harbour engineer, not the sea defence engineer, the pressure exerted by the clapotis is about equal to that which would result from still water against the wall raised to the same height as the top of the clapotis (see Section 1.17; and for more precise theory, see Shore Protection Manual,[13] 7.32, Nonbreaking Wave Forces on Walls). But if air is trapped, other pressures can be developed.[43]

Very intense pressures can occur when a wave breaks against a vertical or near vertical wall enclosing a small pocket of air. The initial shock pressure is similar to water-hammer in pipes. It is of high peak, and model and field investigations show it can be 25 or more times wH_o where H_o is the deep sea wave height, and of short duration, that is, hundredths of a second, and limited to a small area of the wall between still water level and the crest of the breaking wave. Because of this, in most cases, these high pressures need not be taken into account in stability studies of walls. The pressure is proportional to the cube root of the wave energy and increases with wave height and wave length. Model tests by Garcia[44] showed that the depth of water in which waves would break on an unobstructed beach is slightly greater than the depth of water at the wall which would cause the same waves to break and produce maximum shock pressures. (See also reference 45.)

The initial shock pressure is followed by a secondary pressure lasting two seconds or so on the prototype which, Garcia's experiments indicated, was almost identical to the pressures caused by a clapotis formed by the same size wave. However, field measurements by Muraki at Hoboro in Japan indicated that the secondary pressure was more of the order of one-third the initial pressure.

1.20 MOMENTUM METHODS OF ASSESSING WAVE PRESSURES ON WALLS

Sea defence and coast protection engineers are usually mainly concerned with the situation where the breaking wave swashes up an apron of slope 2 : 1 to 4 : 1 and with change of momentum exerts pressure on a wave wall at the top of the slope. For walls of this kind, a momentum approach to determine wave pressure is more usual than wave pressure model studies of the profile.

An early momentum approach to the problem is that of D. H. Little. He gave, using metric units, the velocity of the waves breaking in shallow water as $3.2\sqrt{D_1}$, where D_1 is the height of the crest above the sea bed in metres; and by analogy with the force exerted by change of momentum as a result of a jet of water impinging on a plate, he derived a simple expression which in metric units gives $p = 3.59H$ for the pressure* in Mg/m^2 exerted by breaking waves on maritime works. This formula is applicable to the most usual case of short waves and beach and wall slopes exceeding 1 : 50 (vertical : horizontal). To make some allowance for long waves he suggested the use of the expression $p = 4.49H$, H being the deep sea wave height in metres.

In circumstances such as those shown in Fig. 37 where the wave wall causing the main change in momentum is roughly at the same level as the jet of water from the breaking wave and its height is of the right order to change the momentum effectively, then Little's expression is broadly suitable. However, if the jet of water has to rise substantially in level before being deflected by the wave wall, the expression clearly becomes less suitable, for it will be seen that it does not take into account the elevation of the wave wall in relation to the breaking wave, nor the height of the wave wall in relation to the depth of the swash, nor the hydrostatic pressure. Nevertheless, Little's expression is still of use for rough initial assessments, and wave pressures corresponding to various wave heights may be read from Design Chart N.

A more rigorous approach that does take into account these factors and which should be used in the final design, is as

---

* Multiply by g, i.e. 9.81, to convert to kN.

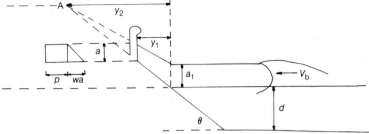

Fig. 7. Momentum method of determining wave pressure on a wave wall

follows. Referring to Fig. 7, the sloping apron of the sea wall is first extended upwards to point A, the estimated swash height if the slope were so extended and if the wave wall did not exist, determined by the methods described in Section 1.18.

Then, velocity at y_1

$$V_{y_1} = V_b - \frac{V_b y_1}{y_2} = V_b \left(1 - \frac{y_1}{y_2}\right)$$

Dynamic pressure on the wall on a in weight units is

$$p = \frac{w V_{y_1}^2}{g} \cos \theta$$

But in shallow water $V_b = \sqrt{(gd)}$, hence

$$p = wd \left(1 - \frac{y_1}{y_2}\right)^2 \cos \theta$$

where V_b = wave velocity, and d = depth of water over foreshore in front of the wall.

To this must be added the triangular static pressure to give the total force acting on the wall over the area a, as shown in Fig. 7.

If the angle of incidence of the waves is α, then the dynamic pressure as calculated must be multiplied by $\cos \alpha$.

To find a, we must first find a_1. The relationship between deep sea wave height H_o and d_b the breaking depth can be taken as

$$H_o = 2.23 d_b (H_0/T^2)^{1/3}$$

Having thus found d_b, the height of the breaking wave H_b may be found by taking d_b equal to $1.28 H_b$. Then, following American practice in this connection, by assuming, nominally, 78% of the breaking wave is above still water level, the dimension a_1 is determined.

Where there is a berm, the simplest approach is to take this into account in determining the height of A and then, otherwise ignoring the berm, carry out the calculation as in Fig. 7 and as just described.

It will be appreciated that in many cases the swash from the previous wave returning to sea will reduce the swash velocity and hence reduce the wave pressures.

There is also the matter of pressures caused by the actual breaking of the wave on the sloping apron. It is shown in Section 4.5 that waves of the order of 0.7 m high are capable of removing 300 mm concrete cubes at the point where the waves plunge. More research in this field is needed; however, it has been found by Skladnev and Popov[46] that for a 4 : 1 slope the ratio p_m/wH varied from about 1.4 for an H/L value of 0.1 to 2.0 for an H/L value of about 0.03, H and L being the inshore wave height and length respectively and p_m the maximum pressure exerted.

1.21   INSTRUMENTATION

When dealing with natural forces it is difficult to predict their effect. Increasing attempts have been made in the field of maritime engineering to establish the parameters on which schemes should be designed. The need to do this accurately is now fully recognised. Few designers have the luxury of comprehensive records of the extent and effect of natural forces on the site or area involved. Many are confronted with a problem which requires an urgent solution, but this should not inhibit them from examining in detail whatever relevant records exist. Opportunity should be taken to set up an adequate recording system for the future. It must be realised that sea defence schemes are expensive and that the establishment of design parameters can make schemes more cost effective.

The principal design components required in any sea defence scheme are the still water levels, wind directions, wind speeds and wave heights. Wind and still water levels can be simply measured. Fig. 8 shows an installation which obtains

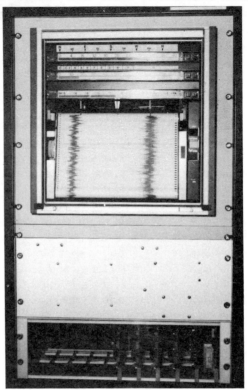

Fig. 8. Wind and tide recorder

and records wind speed and direction, together with tide height. It is situated at Whitstable, with remote reading facilities at Canterbury, some 20 km away. The instrument consists of a base station receiving signals from a wind measuring head located on a mast. Tide height is received from a remote gauge belonging to the Port of London Authority, who gave permission for the use of its radio transmissions. The gauge is of a drum type and is located on a World War II coastal defence tower some 10 km from the shore. (This part of the installation could be replaced by a locally sited drum gauge.) Readings are transmitted via a land link to the base station where they are permanently recorded on a drum recorder. A facility also exists for the interrogation of the unit by telephone to allow access out of working hours to the data being recorded.

32

Fig. 9.   Wave recorder pressure cell

The Institute of Oceanographic Sciences, through the Tide Gauge Inspectorate, can give valuable advice on the types of gauge available. Data obtained from equipment similar to the type described are not restricted to use in design, but also allow for local interpretation of sea storms, giving valuable warning of extreme conditions to areas at risk.

The question of wave height and period is more difficult. The designer needs to know the particular wave climate affecting the scheme under consideration. Valuable data may be obtained from a wave gauge (a graduated pole erected on the foreshore) from which the height of the waves may be estimated. The wave period can be determined by timing with a stopwatch the rise and fall of patches of foam or of the surface of the sea at the wave gauge. This method is only recommended when it is impossible to install instrumentation. Such a climate of observation can take years to obtain and analyse.

Again the Hydraulics Research Station and the Institute of Oceanographic Sciences[48] can provide advice on the type of recording system best suited to the problem of the designer both for this country and other parts of the world.

Fig. 9 shows a wave recorder installed off Whitstable to

determine the local wave climate. The spectra affecting this site are particular to this site and the theoretical predictions made needed confirmation. As the site is tidal it was decided to use a pressure cell recorder located approximately 1 km offshore; this recorder is mounted on a tripod and is located on the sea bed. Signals are transmitted to a receiver via a land line laid along the sea bed to the shore. The receiver records both on cassette and on paper trace the wave data occurring. The data cassette is sent to the Institute of Oceanographic Sciences for analysis by computer.

As an alternative to the pressure cell land line system, and where it is not possible to lay land line data links, the waverider radio transmission system can be used. This equipment transmits data by radio to the base station allowing the remote siting of the instrument from its base.

One area where accurate data collection can aid the designer and can be obtained is that of foreshore movement. Here it is essential to record at frequent intervals the behaviour of the foreshore. One simple guide is the regular taking of level cross-sections at given locations to a constant datum. Such records, when combined with wind data, can provide the designer with accurate information on beach movement trends. From this information the point of maximum run-up can be determined, together with likely beach crest heights and gradients. These assist the designer when considering the provision of groynes within the foreshore. As an alternative to taking levels by conventional means, and if large lengths of coastline are affected, the data may be obtained using aerial survey methods. Such methods must be used with caution, taking into account the tolerances of accuracy available. However, if general trends are required this method is very suitable for use by the designer.

Where a problem requires the accurate determination of beach particle movements other techniques of tracers exist (see Section 2.5). *Beaches and Coasts* by King[2] will provide further detailed information on the methods available. Another excellent reference is Routine Sea Wave Measurement—A Survey[47] which examines and reviews methods for the measurement of sea waves.

REFERENCES

1 THE HYDROGRAPHER OF THE ROYAL NAVY. *Admiralty Tide Tables*. Published annually.

2 KING C. A. M. *Beaches and Coasts*. London, Arnold, 1972.

3 BLACKMAN D. L. and GRAFF J. The analysis of annual extreme sea levels at certain ports in southern England. *Proc. Instn Civ. Engrs*, Part 2, 1978, **65,** June, 339–357.

4 GRAFF J. and BLACKMAN D. L. Analysis of maximum sea levels in southern England. *Proc. 16th Int. Conf. Coastal Engineering, Hamburg*, 1978.

5 GRAFF J. *An Investigation of Frequency Distributions of Annual Sea Level Maxima at Ports around Great Britain*. Birkenhead, Institute of Oceanographic Sciences, 1980.

6 SUTHONS C. T. Frequency of occurrence of abnormally high sea levels on the east and south coasts of England. *Proc. Instn Civ. Engrs*, 1963, **25,** August, 433–450.

7 LENNON G. W. A frequency investigation of abnormally high tidal levels at certain West Coast ports. *Proc. Instn Civ. Engrs*, 1963, **25,** August, 451–484.

8 JENKINSON A. F. Frequency distribution of the annual maximum (or minimum) values of meteorological events. *Q. Jl R. Met. Soc.*, 1955, **81,** 158–177.

9 BLACKMAN D. L. and GRAFF J. The analysis of annual extreme sea levels at ports in southern England. *Proc. Instn Civ. Engrs*, 1978, Part 2, **65,** June, 339–357.

10 ACKERS P. and RUXTON T. D. Extreme levels arising from meteorological surges. *Proc. 14th Int. Conf. Coastal Engineering, Copenhagen*, 1974.

11 PUGH D. T. and VASSIE J. M. *Applications of the Joint Probability Method for Extreme Sea Level Computations*. Birkenhead, Institute of Oceanographic Sciences, 1980.

12 PUGH D. T. and VASSIE J. M. Extreme sea levels from tide and surge probability. *Proc. 16th Int. Conf. Coastal Engineering, Hamburg*, 1978.

13 US ARMY COASTAL ENGINEERING RESEARCH CENTER. *Shore Protection Manual*. Washington, US Government, 1975.

14 BRETSCHNEIDER C. L. *Wave Variability and Wave Spectra for Wind-generated Gravity Waves*. Technical memo 118.

Washington, US Army Corps of Engineers, Beach Erosion Board, 1959.

15 THOMPSON D. M. and SHUTTLER R. M. *Design of Riprap Slope Protection against Wind Waves*. Report 61. London, Construction Industry Research and Information Association, 1976.

16 BRETSCHNEIDER C. L. and REID R. O. *Modification of Wave Height due to Bottom Friction, Percolation and Refraction*. Technical memo 45. Washington, US Army Corps of Engineers, Beach Erosion Board.

17 US ARMY COASTAL ENGINEERING RESEARCH CENTER. *Shore Protection Manual*, 7.121, breaking waves. Washington, US Government, 1975.

18 BRITISH STANDARDS INSTITUTION. *Code of Practice on Maritime Structures*, part 1, section 2. London, British Standards Institution (in draft).

19 ABERNETHY C. L. and GILBERT G. *Refraction of Wave Spectra*. Publication INT 117. Wallingford, Hydraulics Research Station, 1975.

20 HYDRAULICS RESEARCH STATION. *Wave Refraction Programme: Listing and Users' Notes*. Publication INT 131. Wallingford, Hydraulics Research Station, 1975.

21 HYDRAULICS RESEARCH STATION. *Wave Action at Chesil Beach, near Portland Bill*. Report EX 920. Wallingford, Hydraulics Research Station, 1980.

22 SVERDRUP H. U., MUNK W. H. and BRETSCHNEIDER C. L. SMB method for predicting waves in deep water. In *Shore Protection Manual*, 3.51 (US Army Coastal Engineering Research Center). Washington, US Government, 1975.

23 DARBYSHIRE M. and DRAPER L. Forecasting wind-generated sea waves. *Engineering*, 1963, **195,** April, 482–484.

24 HASSELMAN K. *et al*. A parametric wave prediction model. *J. Phys. Oceanography*, 1976, **6,** No. 2.

25 HYDRAULICS RESEARCH STATION. *Numerical Wave Climate Study for the North Sea* (NORSWAM). Report EX 775. Wallingford, Hydraulics Research Station, 1977.

26 HMSO. *Offshore Structures: Guidance on their Design and Construction*. London, HMSO, 1977.

27 HYDRAULICS RESEARCH STATION. *North Wales Coast Road,*

A55, Llandulas to Aber. Report EX 808. Wallingford, Hydraulics Research Station, 1978.

28 ACKERS P. and RUXTON J. T. D. Extreme levels arising from meteorological surges. *Proc. 14th Int. Conf. Coastal Engineering, Copenhagen,* 1974.

29 HYDRAULICS RESEARCH STATION. *Sheppey Sea Defences, Overtopping Discharges and Return Periods.* Report EX 947. Wallingford, Hydraulics Research Station, 1980.

30 HYDRAULICS RESEARCH STATION. *Fleetwood and Cleveleys Sea Defences.* Report EX 871. Wallingford, Hydraulics Research Station, 1979.

31 BENJAMIN J. R. and CORNELL C. A. *Probability Statistics and Decision for Civil Engineers.* New York, McGraw-Hill, 1970.

32 CHATFIELD C. *Statistics for Technology.* London, Penguin Education, 1970.

33 FUKUDA N., UNO F. and IRIE I. Field observations of wave overtopping of wave absorbing revetment. *Coastal Engineering in Japan* **17**. Committee on coastal engineering, Japanese Society of Civil Engineers.

34 BATTJES J. A. Een Oude Golfoploopformule bezien in het hicht van Modeme Theorieen. *De Ingenieur,* 1970, Nov.

35 BATTJES J. A. Run-up distribution of waves breaking on slopes. *J. WatWay Harb. Div., Am. Soc. Civ. Engrs,* 1971, Feb.

36 US ARMY COASTAL ENGINEERING CENTER. *Prediction of Irregular Wave Run-up.* Report CETA 77–2. Washington, US Army Coastal Engineering Center.

37 STOA P. N. *Wave Run up on Steep Slopes.* Report CETA 79–1. Washington, US Army Coastal Engineering Center.

38 HYDRAULICS RESEARCH STATION. *Hydraulic Design of Sea Dikes.* Publication DE 6. Wallingford, Hydraulics Research Station, 1973.

39 SAVAGE R. P. *Laboratory Wave Run-up on Roughened and Permeable Slopes.* Technical memo 109. Washington, US Army Corps of Engineers, Beach Erosion Board, 1959.

40 THORNDIKE SAVILLE *et al.* Freeboard allowances for waves in inland reservoirs. *J. WatWay Harb. Div., Am. Soc. Civ. Engrs,* 1962, **88,** 102.

41 TECHNICAL ADVISORY COMMITTEE ON PROTECTION AGAINST INUNDATION. *Wave Run-up and Overtopping.* The

Hague, Netherlands Government Publishing Office, 1974.

42 AHRENS J. P. and TITUS M. F. Irregular wave run-up and overtopping. *J. WatWays, Port, Coastal, Ocean Div., Am. Soc. Civ. Engrs*, 1978, Nov.

43 RAMKEMA C. A model law for wave impacts on coastal structures. *Proc. 16th Int. Conf. Coastal Engineering, Hamburg*, 1978.

44 GARCIA W. J. *An Experimental Study of Breaking-wave Pressures*. Washington, US Army Engineers Waterways Experimental Station, Corps of Engineers, 1968.

45 GRAVESEN H. and LUNDGREN H. Forces on vertical and sloping face breakwaters. *Proc. 17th Congr. Int. Assoc. Hydraul. Res.*, 1977.

46 SKLADNEV and POPOV. Quoted in *Coastal Engineering*, Vol. 1, 388 (R. Silvester). Amsterdam, Elsevier Scientific Publishing, 1974.

47 DRAPER L. Routine sea wave measurement—a survey. *Underwat. Sci. Techn. Jl*, 1970, 81–86.

48 DRIVER J. S. *A Guide to Sea Wave Recording*. Report No. 103. Marine information advisory service, IOS Wormley.

Chapter 2

Natural sea defences

2.1 GENERAL

A characteristic of sand and shingle foreshores is permeability, which is an important factor in foreshore stability. Any impermeable surface introduced tends to alter this stability and hence the advisability of using, when possible, permeable defences where artificial works are required to aid, strengthen and supplement natural foreshores. Permeable groynes (Figs. 12 and 13) are an example of transverse structure of this kind, and wave screens (Fig. 52), tetrapod walls (Fig. 71), riprap (Fig. 70) and similar permeable revetments (see Section 6.3) are examples of longitudinal ones.

The maintenance and strengthening of natural sea defences are the first aims of the sea defence engineer. Indeed, unless the foreshore can be (or becomes) stabilised by one means or another, there is no end to the additional works required on a sea wall as the foreshore drops, exposing the toe, and as the greater depths of water in front of the wall allow bigger waves to break with greater impact on it.

2.2 EFFECTS OF WAVES AND UNDERWATER BANKS

Seawards of the plunge line (where the waves break), shingle on the bed is not generally moved by waves in depths much greater then the wave height, although it can of course be moved by strong tidal streams in greater depths. However, sand on the bed is moved by waves for a considerable distance offshore, the distance depending on the depth of the water, the grain size, the height and period of the waves.

Long low waves cause a net landward drift along the bed and a net seaward drift at the surface. An onshore wind moving the sea surface landwards will tend to cause an offshore drift on the bed, particularly where the waves are steep. Thus it is that sand foreshores usually accrete during the summer months under the, influence of long low waves and drop during the winter under the action of steep storm waves with onshore winds. As will be seen later, the sand that is drawn down under these conditions is drawn into an area where the rate of littoral drift is much less than on the upper part of the foreshore, so that under subsequent favourable conditions it will tend to return to the upper foreshore.

A feature associated with sand foreshores is the formation of sand bars above the general line of the foreshore slope, roughly in the vicinity of the plunge line at low water. As has already been mentioned, generally these increase during the winter months as the foreshore is drawn down by storm conditions and decrease as the foreshore is built up again under summer conditions.

The effect of offshore underwater banks is to absorb some of the wave energy approaching the coast and to alter to some extent tidal currents. If the water over them is sufficiently shallow (see Section 1.11) waves will break on them and reform at lower wave heights. Hence dredging of such banks could cause larger waves to approach the coast and thereby worsen conditions on the foreshore and defences.

Furthermore, changes of depth caused by dredging could also alter refraction effects (see Section 1.12) and hence, by altering the approach angle of the waves, alter the littoral drift patterns, possibly leading to undesirable erosion and accretion. Mathematical model investigations by the Hydraulics Research Station indicate that for the North Sea coast, the effects of refraction are small in water depths greater than 14m, corresponding very roughly to half the wave length of the most common wave period and a fifth of the length of the extreme wave period. Inshore dredging can also adversely affect foreshores by trapping and thereby interrupting movement of sea-bed material. The Hydraulics Research Station recommendations in this respect for sand are given in Section 2.9. In the case of shingle, they recommend, from studies for the south coast of England, that dredging should not take place in depths less than 18 m below low water.

From the foregoing it will be seen that the chief cause of

movement of sand and shingle is the breaking wave, so that the main movement is above low water and along the foreshore in the direction of the breaking wave, the sand being carried partly in suspension and partly along the bed and the shingle mainly by rolling along the bed. In the case of sand, considerable movement can also be caused by the action of the wind on the exposed dry portion of the surface. The height to which the swash rises and carries the shingle is discussed in Section 1.18. Since the beach is permeable, far less water returns down the surface than goes up it, so that the effect of swash is to build up the shingle. The slope appears therefore to some degree to be a function of the permeability, the less permeable the material, the flatter the slope; thus, the slope of shingle may be 1 in 7 while that of sand may be of the order of 1 in 25, or 1 in 50 (see reference 1).

2.3 EFFECT OF IMPERMEABLE STRUCTURES

In Section 2.2 it was seen that broadly the less permeable the material, the flatter the slope. The effect of impermeable structures has therefore to be carefully considered.

In an experiment carried out by Bagnold,[2] beach material was heaped against a vertical concrete back wall and the wave height was gradually increased until the water surging up the beach reached the vicinity of the wall. It was found that the presence of the wall caused a breakdown to occur before the free water of the surge actually touched the wall above the shingle, the beach breaking down and falling from a slope of 22° to 14°.

In another experiment, a steel plate was inserted at a slope of about 1 in 2 just below the sloping beach surface. It was found to act in the same way as the vertical wall had done, the beach breaking down and falling from a slope of 22° to 14°.

In both cases the changes were evidently caused by the impermeable wall preventing free percolation of the water through the material.

An experiment carried out by Inglis and Russell[3] indicated the effect of vertical walls on sand foreshores. Fine sand was laid and allowed to become stable under the action of waves of constant height and of fluctuating tidal levels of constant range. When the profile had become stable, a vertical plate representing a sea wall was inserted at a point between high water and the highest point reached by the swash. As the experiment continued, the level of the sand against the sea wall fell and after about 35 tides it had fallen from above high-water level to below low-water level.

The effect of an impermeable apron in flattening the slope of shingle is not usually so serious as for sand, since the change in slope is not great and the same total volume of shingle remains in front of the wall to absorb wave impact. As has been seen, in the case of sand, the effect is much more serious, and it appears that the flatter the slope of the wall, the less severe is the disturbance to the foreshore. Further information in this connection is given in Section 4.3.

2.4 LITTORAL DRIFT

Littoral drift, termed littoral transport in the United States, where the material moved is referred to as the littoral drift, is the aggregate movement of material along the coast (in English usage littoral drift can also mean the material moved). Its direction is determined by strength, duration and direction of winds and the fetches corresponding to the wind directions. If the prevailing wind comes from the direction of the shortest fetch, then it is unlikely that the direction of the drift will be that of the prevailing wind.

On the south coast of England, the prevailing wind comes from the south west and, as this is also the direction of the longest fetch, the littoral drift is generally eastward. The rate of drift is naturally affected by the angle of the coastline to the waves. A reverse movement may, however, prevail, for instance where a land promontory gives protection from the west. This phenomenon is created by the shingle promontory of Dungeness in Kent, so that the drift is south westward between Littlestone and Greatstone, which are on the east side of Dungeness. On the east coast of England the drift has in the past been predominantly southerly.

In some circumstances it could be possible for the shingle drift to be in one direction and the sand drift in the other (in the case of sand drift, the movement of sand by the wind must, of course, never be overlooked, see Section 2.10). For example, because of the shielding effect of a headland or because the fetch is short, only small waves may reach a shore from the direction of the prevailing wind, and these would move sand but not shingle. Winds from opposing directions, on the other hand, may generate larger waves and therefore cause shingle drift in the direction opposite to that of the net sand drift.

The drift does not necessarily cause erosion of the foreshore—it may equally cause accretion; it is changes in the rate of drift that are significant. Since the angle of the waves to the shore affects the rate of drift, there will be a tendency for erosion or accretion to occur where the line of the shore changes direction. The determining factors are the rate of arrival and the rate of departure of beach material over the length of foreshore considered. Coast erosion by wave action is not always the only source of foreshore material, for some evidence suggests it is possible in particular circumstances for strong tidal currents to feed beaches from offshore. Similarly there is evidence that in some circumstances, shingle can be 'lost' into sand lying seaward of the toe of the shingle bank.

Littoral drift of both sand and shingle can exhibit an undulating character, that is to say a large body of material in the form of a hump can move along the coast.

2.5   RATE OF LITTORAL DRIFT AND SHORELINE CHANGES

It will be appreciated that a net littoral drift in one direction often results from large movements in both directions. The effect of groynes or other obstructions can give a good indication of net littoral drift, either from the rate of accumulation at the obstruction, or from the down-drift erosion caused.

Dealing first with shingle, a good example of this is the Pett foreshore on the south coast just west of Rye. There is virtually no supply of shingle reaching the frontage from the west and at its eastern end, the western arm of Rye Harbour collects all the shingle and prevents it from blocking the mouth of the River Rother. The beach is maintained by taking shingle from where it is accreting at the eastern end and with it replenishing the beach to the west where erosion occurs. After a year the increase in the accumulation on the west side of the western arm, added to the quantities removed over the year, is a measure of the littoral drift.

Similarly, where along a length a new system of groynes has been constructed, initially greatly reducing the littoral drift, some assessment of the magnitude of littoral drift can be made by comparing the foreshore change down-drift of the groyne system before and after construction of the groynes and/or assessing the quantities retained by the groynes.

Where these means of estimating littoral drift are not possible, as an alternative, fluorescent tracers of material similar to the shingle may be used by a method developed by the Hydraulics Research Station.[4]

If the drift were at a constant rate of d tonnes a day and t tonnes of tracers were added each day, then the concentration of tracers would be t/d. However, drift is not at a constant rate. If, therefore, the beach is divided into equal compartments and it is assumed that each contains C tonnes of 'moving' shingle and that in one week xC tonnes moves into the next compartment on one side and yC tonnes moves into the compartment on the other side, $x + y = 1$, with x equal to or greater than y, then the net drift in one week is $(x - y)C$ tonnes, or $52(x - y)C$ tonnes in one year. The concentration of tracers K_{zi} in any compartment, z compartments from the injection point after i injections, is the total weight of tracers in the compartment Q_{zi} divided by C. Thus $K_{zi} = Q_{zi}/C$, or $C = Q_{zi}/K_{zi}$ from which the net drift per year is $52(x - y)Q_{zi}/K_{zi}$.

If it is assumed that 1 tonne of tracers is injected each time, then for various values of z and i, Q_{zi} can be found. For a given number of injections, graphs are then plotted of Q_{zi} (for 1 tonne of tracers per injection) against compartment numbers for various values of x. The actual value of x (and hence y) can then be found by comparing the shape of the actual concentration curve with the plotted graphs; Q_{zi} is taken from the graph and K_{zi} is measured on the beach; hence from the given expression the net drift per year can be calculated.

The tracer pebbles are made from heavy (quartz dolerite) concrete of the same density as the shingle, in which are imbedded fragments of fluorescent plastic. A typical rate of injection is 350 kg per week. Surveys counting the number of tracers on the surface are made at night at time of low water by means of a portable generator and ultra-violet lamp, with square frames laid on the beach. From the results and from calibration tests of various concentrations of tracers and shingle giving the number of tracers visible for given concentrations, the values of K_{zi} on the beach are determined (see references 4 and 5).

A recent development is the use of metal tracer pebbles of specific gravity, size and shape similar to the beach pebbles. Whereas fluorescent tracers can only be detected on the surface, metal tracers can be detected by metal detectors both on and under the surface.[6]

The Hydraulics Research Station[7] give the following expression, based on the Scripps/Komar equation and on investigations on the south coast of England, for the rate of alongshore transport of shingle due to waves in the absence of tidal currents:

$$Q = 0.035 \, E \, nC \sin 2a/y_s$$

where Q = volumetric rate of alongshore transport, in cubic metres of dry material per year; y_s = submerged unit weight of beach material in place (in N/m^3); nC = group velocity of breaking waves (which in shallow water is equal to the velocity of single waves); a = angle between the breaking wave front and the shoreline; $E = \rho g H_b^2/8$, i.e. energy density of the breaking waves; ρ = mass density of sea water; g = acceleration due to gravity; and H_b = wave height, from trough to crest, at breaking.

The Hydraulics Research Station has developed a numerical model based on the alongshore transport expressions given in this Section for shingle and sand to predict changes in the plan shape of beaches resulting from the construction of long groynes, harbour arms, or the changes in wave climate following offshore dredging.[8]

However, generally in sea defence and coast protection works, one is more concerned with the rates of erosion or accretion on lengths of foreshore, and here, net average rate of loss or gain of beach can be assessed from a survey programme of regular cross-sectioning. For more extensive studies, covering several or many miles of coast, it is sometimes more appropriate to use regular aerial photogrammetric surveys. This is especially so for shingle, for which the method is more accurate than for sand (for which in many cases aerial survey would not be sufficiently accurate).

Considering now the rate of littoral drift on sand foreshores, the methods to be adopted are basically the same as described for shingle, including the use of fluorescent tracers.

The Hydraulics Research Station expression given in this Section may also be used to determine the rate of alongshore transport of sand, by waves, provided the dimensionless constant 0.035 is changed to 0.385 (the Scripps/Komar equation). Alternatively, the Shore Protection Manual (Chapter 1, reference 13) offers a somewhat similar method based on using measured or calculated wave conditions to compute the longshore component of wave energy flux (energy density times group velocity, per unit wave crest width) and relating this through an empirical curve to longshore transport rate (Chapter 1, reference 13, section 4.53, Longshore Transport Rate).

With sand (and in some cases with shingle) there is the complication of onshore-offshore movement which should, if possible, be taken into account. The Hydraulics Research Station numerical model referred to above can do this if the quantity is known. (See also reference 9.)

2.6 GROYNES

It was seen in Section 2.2 that the movement of material along the coast affecting the foreshore is mainly above low water. It is greatest in the vicinity of high water, and hence causes one of the difficulties of accreting sand on low foreshores at levels where the rate of movement is much less. Groynes are used to limit the movement of material and to stabilise the foreshore. They combat erosion and encourage accretion. It is generally impracticable to construct groynes that will halt all drift and since, therefore, normal groynes cannot prevent all loss of material, in the long run they are useless unless natural or artificial feed is available to replace the material that is lost. With limited feed, high groynes usually have the effect of forming the shingle bank very irregularly and from the amenity aspect they are disadvantageous. They are also costly and consequently, low groynes are more usual these days for shingle as well as for sand foreshores.

On shingle beaches, the head of the groyne is preferably taken either a short distance landward of the shingle full or into the sea wall, while on sand foreshores where the sand is usually well below high water,the landward end of the groyne terminates at the lower part of the sea wall.

Where the groynes are used to hold shingle, they are carried seawards only a short distance beyond the toe of the shingle. The distance seawards that groynes designed to hold sand are extended depends on the feed and the build-up required. If the feed is not great, they are taken down to low water in order to trap as much material as possible; if the feed is good, they can sometimes be made a little shorter, particularly if the build-up required is small, otherwise the groyne will not be long enough to provide the gradient needed for the build-up at the landward end. Unless special circumstances exist, in practice, low water is taken to be low-water neap tides. The cost of groyne construction greatly increases seaward of low-water neaps.

The cumulative effect of the normal type of solid groyne is to build up material on the side from which the material is coming and to cause erosion on the other side until the accretion tops the groyne and material passes over (or round the seaward end) to commence filling the next compartment. In calm conditions, with small, directly onshore waves, the effect on a sand foreshore is to even up the distribution of sand within the groyne compartments.

The Hydraulics Research Station basic coastal model represented an idealised version of the foreshore to the south of Southwold Harbour and the results are qualitatively applicable to prototype sands ranging from 0.15 to 0.45 mm mean grain size (on the Dymchurch foreshore in Kent, the sand ranges from about 0.125 to 0.33 mm, being mainly about 0.17 mm). The results of the experiments apply best to foreshores where the sand is somewhat coarser than that typically found on British coasts.

Solid groynes 1 m high, 55 m long and 55 m apart reduced the quantity of littoral drift to one eighth of its former value, but also resulted in a loss of sand from the upper part of the foreshore. Solid groynes 0.5 m high, 55 m long and 110 m apart reduced the littoral drift to half and did not cause a loss of sand

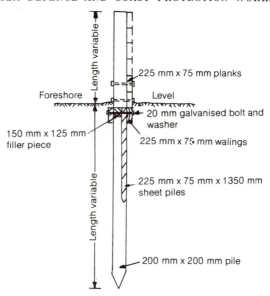

Fig. 10. *Details of Kent type groyne*

from the upper foreshore. It was found that there was no loss of sand if the sand built up to the top of the groynes, but that if the sand did not do this, then a loss occurred. It was therefore inferred that for the conditions reproduced in the experiments, low, widely spaced groynes were to be preferred.

In some of the experiments, there was a loss of sand from the foreshore and a corresponding accumulation offshore. In no case was there a gain of sand and a corresponding loss offshore.

The experiments were made with waves the equivalent of 0.6 m high in deep water which rose to 1 m before breaking and always approached obliquely from the same direction. The tidal range reproduced was 2 m and the tidal currrents reached a maximum equivalent to 0.6 m/s in both directions.

The Hydraulics Research Station investigations showed that the quantity of littoral drift was greatest in the vicinity of the high water contour and less than one tenth of that quantity along the low water contour.

With the very flat slope of sand (as distinct from that of shingle), it must always be borne in mind that the effect of

48

Fig. 11.   Groyne with land ties

groynes where they accrete at very low levels must be to lay the sand at artificially steep slopes. It must be frankly admitted that the way groynes affect low sand foreshores (if indeed in many cases there is any material effect) is obscure.

Groynes are commonly constructed at right angles to the shore and at spacings equal to their lengths. The angle and the spacing on any foreshore eventually become fixed as the result of long experience determining the most efficient arrangement. Shorter intermediate groynes are often placed between the main groynes. On foreshores where there has been no previous experience of groyning works, it is, as a general rule, better to commence with groynes at spacings equal to one and a half times to twice the length of the groynes and to later increase the number of groynes, if necessary, in the light of the results obtained.

In the tests carried out by the Hydraulics Research Station, with the groynes aligned at an angle of 18° from the normal, with their offshore ends in the 'down-drift' direction, no measurable difference was found from the experiment with the groynes normal to the shore. With the groynes pointing towards the origin of the littoral drift, the results were very similar, except that erosion down-drift of each groyne was

49

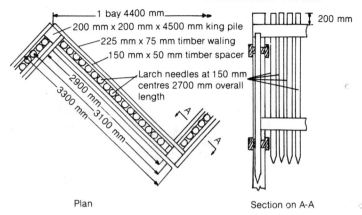

Fig. 12. Details of permeable timber groyne

greater than with normal groynes and this tended to endanger the stability of the groynes (a further reference on littoral drift and groynes is reference 10).

Construction of groynes is normally commenced at the end furthest from the direction from which the feed is coming. Where possible, it is advisable to begin the construction on a length where accretion is taking place, in order to reduce the problem of the terminal groyne to a minimum. To allow the foreshore to build up relatively uniformly, it is customary to begin with no more than two planks at each groyne above foreshore level and to plank up one or two boards at a time above the material as the foreshore accretes. Artificial replenishment down-drift of the terminal groyne will generally be necessary, at least until the groyne compartments are filled; alternatively, the new groyne compartments can be filled (see Sections 2.7 and 2.9). Within the groyne compartments, the material tends to become orientated so that it faces the on-coming waves directly.

Fig. 10 gives details of a timber groyne developed in Kent that has proved popular for both sand and shingle foreshores. The timber sheet piles are to prevent under-run.

Under very exposed conditions, land ties are sometimes used to strengthen groynes and Fig. 11 illustrates the use of these at Eastbourne on a shingle beach.

50

Fig. 13.   Timber permeable groyne

Salt water prevents attack by fungi (except marine fungi which only slightly soften and do not seriously harm the wood) so that the qualities that have to be borne in mind in choosing suitable timbers are resistance to abrasion (particularly on shingle beaches), resistance to marine borers (where these are present), ease of working and cost. The hardwoods jarrah, greenheart and oak are resistant to abrasion and to some extent to attack by marine borers, but are less easy to work than softwoods. Pine is a popular soft-wood for groyne construction; it is cheap, easy to work and is suitable for sand foreshores where it will not be subjected to much shingle abrasion. If the presence of marine borers is known or suspected, softwoods can be made resistant to attack by pressure creosoting (incised full cell process) or by similar treatment with proprietary chemical preservatives. The latter have the advantage that the timber is 'clean' for handling after treatment.

A number of timber permeable groynes have been constructed on shingle foreshores on the east and south coasts of Kent (Figs. 12 and 13). These groynes have the effect of retarding the longitudinal velocity component of the breaking wave and the swash and hence slowing down the rate of littoral movement. Unlike conventional solid groynes, while they impede the shingle drift, at the same time they allow some pebbles to pass

51

through, and so reduce scour on the sides remote from the direction from which the material is coming. The effect is then to build up the beach for considerable distances on either side of the groyne.

In general, these groynes are not superior to conventional solid groynes, but in some particular circumstances their use may be preferred: for example, on very exposed positions where there may be a danger of conventional groynes being damaged and washed out, or on very isolated lengths where the cost of planking and deplanking conventional groynes would be excessive, or as terminal groynes combined, as necessary, with artificial feed where the typical scour created on the down-drift side of solid groynes would not be acceptable.

No permeable groynes on sand foreshores have been built in Kent, but they were constructed on the Norfolk coast by the late S. W. Mobbs, the pioneer in this field. For example, some were constructed at Mundesley in 1958 in conjunction with a permeable revetment, and it was reported that within a short time this foreshore attained a level 1.2 m above the 1953 level.

Results of model tests at the Hydraulics Research Station on permeable groynes for sand foreshores were not encouraging. Hydraulics Research Paper No 3[10] says 'According to Mr Mobbs the accumulation begins several hundred feet up-drift of the first groyne raising a bar of fine sand near the low water-mark, which extends along the system. The bar moves slowly inshore to build up the upper beach. This behaviour could not have been reproduced in the model at HRS because the zone where the accumulation might first have taken place was outside the limits of the model.' A summary of current groyne practice is given in HRS Report[13] 1T199.

2.7 BEACH RECHARGE (SHINGLE FEED) SCHEMES

Artificial building up and feeding of shingle provides a natural permeable defence, and if the annual replenishment required is not too great, it will often be found that the initial cost plus the capitalised cost of annual replenishment is much less than the sum of the corresponding costs for a sea wall improvement which would be an alternative type of sea defence.

Under these schemes, material is transported from where shingle is accreting to lengths where erosion is taking place.

Fig. 14. Shingle being tipped

The replenishment shingle benefits not only the section of coast where it is placed, but also the down-drift coast along which it eventually travels.

It should be borne in mind that unless an eroding foreshore in front of a sea wall is stabilised, the inevitable prospect of repeatedly extending the apron of the wall seawards as the foreshore falls must be faced. As the toe of the wall becomes exposed, there is usually the added threat that with the greater depths of water in front, larger waves can break on the wall, with greater impact and uprush. Generally speaking, on a deteriorating foreshore, shingle drops much more rapidly than sand, and the estimated rate of fall determines the extent to which an apron should be extended. For example, if the shingle is dropping rapidly, then the apron should be extended to at least sand level.

Artificial replenishment has been carried out for many years on the Pett and Walland foreshores in Sussex. For the initial placing, the shingle was tipped on the foreshores down to low water at intervals along the shore up to about 300 metres and to roughly the final level of the top of the reformed bank (see Fig. 14). The action of the sea then distributed it along the beach, leaving little to be moved by machine. This is only possible where, as at these sites, there is a reasonably strong littoral

53

Fig. 15. Beach recharge at Sheerness; split-bottom barge and tug in background

movement, annual replenishment along the 4 km length at Walland being of the order of 31 000 m³. However, at Sheerness, where the littoral movement is not strong, the forming of the bank was by machine.

The Pett and Walland schemes were carried out using onshore material. In the case of the Sheerness scheme, in 1975, 180 000 m³ of shingle were dredged off the bed of the North Sea, transported in 1000 tonne, 600 tonne and 350 tonne split-bottom barges and dumped at high water on the foreshore (Fig. 15).

As far as is known, this was the first time shingle recharge was carried out in this manner. At low water, the material was placed by draglines and bulldozers to the design profile, for, unlike the case of the Walland foreshore, movement of shingle along this foreshore is small and occurs mainly during the winter months. As this scheme had to be completed during the summer, the prevailing south westerly wind with a good fetch was not available in this case to give a helping hand, as Sheerness is on the north coast.

The Walland and Sheerness schemes were full beach recharge schemes and the design of such schemes is described

54

in Section 2.8. In such cases, no groynes are needed. However, for partial beach recharge schemes, carried out to give increased protection to existing sea walls by increasing the quantity of shingle in front of them, groynes are necessary to limit as far as possible the movement of the shingle. They inevitably produce the saw-tooth configuration of the beach in plan which is so distinct from the smooth appearance of full beach recharge schemes.

2.8 DESIGN OF BEACH RECHARGE SCHEMES

Methods of estimating rates of littoral drift are set out in Section 2.5.

Provided there is enough shingle, the higher the tide and the higher the waves, the more the sea will build up the shingle to defeat itself. In passing, this is an example of the principle called in Japanese Ju (believed to be Wu-wei in Chinese), namely that your use your opponent's weight and strength as the means of his defeat. For design it should be assumed that for stability the top of the shingle bank should be at or slightly above swash height and the seaward profile must be at the stable slope of the shingle under design storm conditions, with which are associated flatter slopes than under summer conditions. The design should also incorporate a wide crest to allow for higher than expected swash and flatter than expected slopes under storm conditions.

Sometimes, as in the cases of the Sussex south coast schemes described in Section 2.7, the required information on swash height and stable slopes is provided by adjoining banks of similar shingle size and with similar wave conditions.

A summary of existing knowledge and design recommendations is given by the Hydraulics Research Station in reference 7. This shows that of all the beaches studied, 30% had slopes (measured from crest to seaward toe) between 7:1 and 8:1 and less than 5% were flatter than 10:1. Very few of these were measured following storms and those that were tended to be flatter than during normal conditions. From the Authors' own observations of the Sheerness beach recharge scheme described in Section 2.7, over a period of four years since it was carried out, which includes the worst storm conditions since

1953, it would seem that the stable slope of the beach there under storm condition is 7:1 on some sections and a little flatter on others.

For initially estimating swash height, the Hydraulics Research Station recommendations are given in reference 38, chapter 1 (section 1.18). This deals in detail with (2% exceeding) swash heights on smooth, impermeable seaward slopes. Corrections for roughness and permeability can be made from reference 39, chapter 1. These depend on the size of the shingle, and results suggest reductions of the order of 0.2 due to roughness and 0.5 due to permeability. The Hydraulics Research Station caution that reductions should be used with care, since in some cases high silt and sand content in the shingle could greatly reduce the permeability.

The Hydraulics Research Station advises, for the purposes of estimating shingle quantities, a slope of 10:1 should be assumed and that the crest should be set at the level exceeded by the run-up of the 2% highest storm waves on a smooth, impermeable slope (obtained from their publication DE6, reference 38, chapter 1). In this connection the reader is referred to the Battjes expression explained in Section 1.18.

2.9 SAND REPLENISHMENT SCHEMES

Because of the flatter stable slopes of sand, sand replenishment schemes involve, for the same crest level, far greater quantities of material than in the case of shingle recharge, and if shingle is available, this favours its use. Where, however, shingle is not easily available and sand is, and there are also holiday industry considerations to be taken into account, sand may be the chosen replenishment material.

One example of a sand replenishment scheme is that at Portobello Beach where the Edinburgh Corporation carried out work involving the transfer of 180 000 m^3 of sand from the sea bed well offshore to the shore. At the beginning of the century, the sand foreshore was stable and at a high level. Deterioration seems to have been started by the regular removal of sand for supplying local glass works and exacerbated by the vertical sea wall (effects of vertical sea walls on sand foreshores are dealt with in Section 2.3).

Fig. 16. Bournemouth—foreshore before sand recharge (reproduced by permission Mr R. E. L. Lelliott, Bournemouth Borough Council)

A sloping apron to the wall was built, and while this slowed down the rate of fall of the foreshore, a stage was reached where major works were considered necessary to safeguard the wall. As an alternative to a further extension of the apron, a sand recharge scheme was considered, which had amenity advantages. The matter was referred to the Hydraulics Research Station and the outcome of their investigation was that they considered the foreshore could be restored by sand recharge and stabilised by groynes. Estimates indicated that the cost would be less than that of extending the sea wall apron.

A bucket dredger loaded the sand from the sea into barges that took the sand two or three kilometres to a suction dredger where it was fluidised by a water jet and pumped ashore through a submerged pipeline. Bulldozers shaped the material to the required profile.

The work was carried out over a length of 1.6 km and included the construction of six groynes. The initial foreshore slope of 42:1 of 0.20 mm median size sand was steepened to 20:1 by using a coarser sand of median size 0.27 mm. This

Fig. 17. Bournemouth—foreshore after sand recharge (reproduced by permission HMSO, courtesy Hydraulics Research Station, Wallingford)

design slope of 20:1 was based on the sand sizes and foreshore slopes of neighbouring foreshores of similar wave climate.

Annual cross-section surveys over the first three years showed only relatively small changes and that, within 100 m of the sea wall, the upper levels of the intertidal area, 80% of the material remained at the end of the three years. Some of the remaining sand had spread to the east, but there was no visual evidence of any of the sand having moved off-shore.

On the south coast, a sand replenishment scheme has also been carried out at Bournemouth to maintain the foreshore, but studies indicated that there would be a considerable rate of depletion and subsequent monitoring confirmed this. Loss of sand here is thought to have resulted from other defence works giving protection to an eroding cliff and thus depriving this foreshore of its natural source of nourishment.

Figs. 16 and 17 show the foreshore between Bournemouth and Boscombe piers, looking east before and after sand recharge. The work was carried out over a length of 6.5 km and the median grain size was 0.2 mm. By 1977, about 33% of the

58

material pumped ashore in 1974/5 remained, as did 68% of the material placed just offshore.

Major sand recharge schemes carried out overseas include 4.5 million cubic metres over 38 km in Harrison County, Miss., USA; at the Island of Goeree, Holland, 3.6 million cubic metres over 3 km; at Copacobana-Rio, Brazil, 3.5 million cubic metres over 4.2 km, and at the Island of Norderney, Germany, 1 million cubic metres over 38 km.

The fact that studies indicate considerable rates of depletion does not necessarily invalidate a scheme, it is a matter of cost/benefit. Generally, in the case of seaside towns, where the livelihood of the people depends to a great extent on the holiday industry, the cost of a sand recharge scheme plus the capitalised cost of maintenance replenishment may well be far less than the capitalised value of the losses to the holiday industry which might otherwise occur.

The cost of mobilising the plant required means that for small quantities of material, say of the order of 20 000 m³, sand recharge schemes cannot generally be economically viable. Again, sources of sand further away than say 10 km may also prove too costly. Care must, of course, be taken to ensure that the dredging does not remove the protection given by off-shore underwater sandbanks to foreshores to landward of them. This matter is dealt with in more detail in Section 2.2. Again, if dredging is too near the shore, foreshore draw-down can occur. The Hydraulics Research Station recommend for the United Kingdom in this connection that dredging should not be nearer than 610 m to low water.

A customary procedure is to form a bund with foreshore sand near low water and pump sand into the bund, allowing the water to drain away at the ends of the bund. The delivery pipe can run for a kilometre or so on each side of the supply pipe with valves in each leg. This permits lengthening of one while sand is being delivered through the other.

In time, wave action would form the new grade, but in so doing would form a 'cliff' which might be dangerous to the public. Considerable grading by scrapers and bulldozers is therefore usually necessary.

For a more detailed account of present-day practice, the reader is referred to reference 11. In this paper, the author sum-

Fig. 18.   First line of wattle fencing

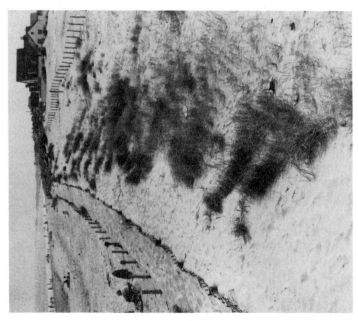

Fig. 19.   First line of wattle fencing buried

Fig. 20.   Second line of wattle fencing

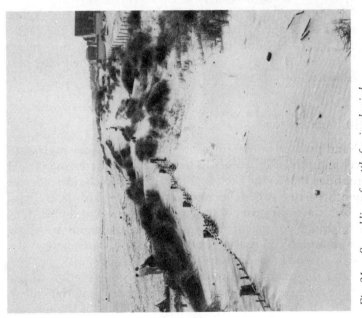

Fig. 21.   Second line of wattle fencing buried

61

marises his recommendations as follows:

(a) a study of the beach, in which the possible causes of the reduced levels may be established, should first be made

(b) replenishment of the beach should be made with a sand coarser than that already existing; a D_{50} size of at least 1½ times the indigenous sand should be aimed at; it may be obtained from inland sources, but when taken from offshore it should not be removed in the nearshore zone; if extracted at distances greater than 10 km offshore the operation may be too costly

(c) sufficient material should be placed ashore to establish a final slope that is compatible with the wave climate; while this may not at present be forecast with accuracy, an examination of neighbouring beaches exposed to a similar wave climate may give a good indication of what should be attempted

(d) in order to avoid the loss of newly won material by littoral drift, the establishment of groyne systems may be advisable; they are particularly useful if severe gales occur during a beach nourishment exercise

(e) after-care of a new beach must include some regular measure of survey of the beach profiles so that the rate of change of volume may be established; by this means 'topping-up' operations may be started when the need arises.

2.10 SAND DUNES

Sand by itself may form a foreshore rising above high water level and this often occurs in bays. It is characteristic of such situations that as the sand is able to dry between tides, it is frequently carried still higher and further shorewards by the wind to form the upper part of the foreshore and sand dunes. Thus an adequate sea defence may be formed and examples on the Sussex and Kent coasts may be seen at Camber, near Rye Harbour, and at Greatstone, just east of Dungeness.

Sand dunes may be built up by the construction of permeable screens. These may be of any suitable material and are usually about 1 m high with a total of about 50% of their area

Fig. 22. *Timber footbridge just after construction*

Fig. 23. *Timber footbridge showing build-up of dunes*

open. As the screens become buried, further screens are constructed above them and so the dune is built up.

To stabilise the dunes, marram grass is planted. Once it is well rooted, it collects wind-blown sand, holds it and gradually builds it up. Marram is unfortunately destroyed by pedestrian traffic; hence the need to fence off dunes where possible to prevent damage by the public. Figs. 18 to 21, of Greatstone sand dunes, were taken from the footbridge in Fig. 22 and show the build-up of sand following the erection of two rows of wattle fencing. Fig. 23 shows the amount of accretion that had taken place over a period of seven years, together with the establishment of marram grass.

The shrub buckthorn grows well on sand dunes, it helps to stabilise the sand and its prickly nature acts as a deterrent to those who might damage the dunes. Conifers have also been grown successfully on sand dunes; they are usually planted about 1.5 m apart at the age of two or three years. Grass seed can also be sown on sand dunes and a description of this is given in Section 2.11.

2.11 GRASS SOWING ON SAND DUNES

Experience in Kent indicates that the best method is to 'disc' in chopped straw to a surface prepared by bulldozing, sow the grass seed hydraulically or by hand and apply a second straw mulch which can be tacked down with bitumen to give added protection. Autumn sowings carried out in this way establish a good grass cover. A high nitrogen content fertiliser, specially prepared to remain effective over periods of nine to twelve months, is applied to provide the necessary nourishment for healthy growth.

The grass seed mixture consists of the following:

34.5 kg S143 Cocksfoot B.C.
9.5 kg Creeping Red Fescue Canadian
1.4 kg Ribgrass
5.4 kg Birdsfoot Trefoil

Grass sown in this way at Camber became well established. Over a period of years, much of the grass on the seaward slope was naturally replaced by marram and on the landward slope was overcome by moss. Since the stabilisation has not been affected, there has been no need to re-seed.

2.12 STABILITY OF FORESHORES IN BAYS

In order to study the equilibrium shape in plan of sand fore-shores (rising above high water level) in bays, Silvester[12] generated waves in model tests at 45° to an initially straight sandy shoreline which incorporated three concrete blocks representing rocky headlands. From the tests he concluded that the equilibrium shape is that of a half-heart (crenulate) with the curved portion at the up-coast end and the tangent section at the down-coast end. Under equilibrium conditions and as a result of refraction and diffraction, the wave orthogon-als are normal to all sections of the foreshore and consequently there is no longshore littoral drift.

His findings are of particular significance for coasts facing open oceans where persistent swell is the dominant factor.

The equilibrium curve is a logarithmic spiral, the equation of which is

$$\frac{R_2}{R_1} = e^{\theta \cot \alpha}$$

where R_1 and R_2 are radii from an origin that are at an angle of θ radians to each other and α is the constant angle of the radii to tangents of the curve. If α for a given curve is known, and an angle for plotting of θ is taken, the equation gives a value of R_2/R_1, and hence the curve can be plotted.

Further model tests of the equilibrium state by Silvester pro-vided a curve (see reference 12) relating α to the approach angle β of the waves to the line joining the headlands. Typical values from the curve are: $\beta = 10°$, $\alpha = 76°$; $\beta = 20°$, $\alpha = 63°$; $\beta = 30°$, $\alpha = 54°$; $\beta = 40°$, $\alpha = 48°$; $\beta = 50°$, $\alpha = 44°$; $\beta = 60°$, $\alpha = 40°$; $\beta = 70°$, $\alpha = 36°$. The model tests covered the range from $\beta = 30°$ to 60°, the remaining results given are therefore extrapol-ated. Three wave periods were used and the results indicated that wave period does not affect the problem.

Hence, given the approach angle, it is possible from this re-lationship to check whether or not a particular bay is in equili-brium.

Fig. 24.   Rice grass on saltings

2.13 SALTINGS

The value of saltings as sea defences is described in Chapter 4. Rice grass (see Fig. 24), is used to combat erosion and to build up saltings in front of clay embankments in order to give increased protection from wave action and to support stone pitching that tends to slip into the soft mud that often exists at the toe of such walls.

Rice grass will not grow well if it is covered by water for more than an average of three to four hours each tide and it seems to thrive best where the roots are covered only by high spring tides. Plants put in one metre apart in the spring usually grow into a compact mass in three to six years.

REFERENCES

1   MAYER R.E. (ed.) *Waves on Beaches and Resulting Sediment Transport*. London, Academic Press, 1972.
2   BAGNOLD R. A. Beach formation by waves. *J. Instn Civ. Engrs*, 1940, **15,** Nov., 27–52.

3   INGLIS C. C. and RUSSELL R. C. H. Influence of a vertical wall on a beach in front of it. *Proceedings of International Hydraulics Convention, Minnesota,* 1953.

4   REID W. J. and JOLLIFFE I. P. Coastal experiments with fluorescent tracers. *Dock and Harbour Authority,* 1961, Feb., 341–345.

5   HYDRAULICS RESEARCH STATION. *Littoral Drift at Deal.* Report EX 178. Wallingford, Hydraulics Research Station, 1962.

6   WRIGHT P. *et al.* Shingle tracing by a new technique. *Proc. 16th Int. Conf. Coastal Engineering, Hamburg,* 1978.

7   HYDRAULICS RESEARCH STATION. *Review of Shingle Sea Defences.* Publication DE 7. Wallingford, Hydraulics Research Station, 1973.

8   PRICE W. A. *et al.* Predicting changes in the plan shape of beaches. *Proc. 13th Int. Conf. Coastal Engineering, Vancouver,* 1972, 1321–1329.

9   WALTON T. L. and CHIU T. Y. A review of analytical techniques to solve the sand transport equation and some simplified solutions. In *Coastal Structures.* New York, American Society of Civil Engineers, 1979.

10 RUSSELL R. C. *Coast Erosion and Defence.* Hydraulics research paper 3. London, HMSO, 1960.

11 NEWMAN D. E. Beach replenishment: sea defences and a review of the role of artificial beach replenishment. *Proc. Instn Civ. Engrs,* Part 1, 1976, **60,** Aug., 445–460.

12 SILVESTER R. *Coastal Engineering,* Vol. 2. Amsterdam, Elsevier Scientific Publishing, 1974.

13 TOMLINSON J. H. *Groynes in coastal engineering.* Report IT199. Wallingford, Hydraulics Research Station, 1980.

Chapter 3

Sea walls, estuary walls and counterwalls

Soil mechanics considerations

3.1 TYPES OF CLAY WALL AND SAND WALL FAILURE

Clay walls may fail owing to one or more of the following causes:

(a) direct frontal erosion by wave action
(b) flow through the fissured zone causing a shallow slump to occur on the landward face of the wall
(c) scour of the back of the wall by overtopping
(d) failure by gravitational slip
(e) delayed slip
(f) failure of landward side of the wall by uplift pressure acting through permeable underlying strata

Walls made of sandy permeable material may fail from causes (a) and (c) and

(g) as a result of seepage drag forces reducing the stability of the wall
(h) by local slumping or local erosion caused by water seeping out above the landward toe of the wall.

3.1.1. Frontal erosion

Protection from direct frontal attack by wave action can only be given by providing a suitable revetment which is described in Chapter 4.

3.1.2. Fissured zone and shallow slumps

A common cause of failure is from flow through the fissured zone. From inspections made by Cooling and Marsland (reported by Marsland[1]) following the floods of 1953, it would

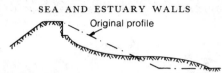

Fig. 25. Shallow slip failure

seem that the major cause of failure in a large proportion of cases was shallow slumps, resulting from flow through the fissured zone. Most clay sea and estuary walls (but not necessarily non-tidal river walls where high water levels may be maintained) have a fissured zone extending to a depth of 1 or 1.25 m below the surface caused by the drying out of the surface and reduction of moisture content resulting from vegetational growth.

At times of exceptional high tide, water flows through the fissures and shallow slumps may result, as illustrated by Fig. 25. If the top width of the wall is narrow, the effect of the slump will often be to reduce the height, width and strength of that part of the wall to such an extent that a breach and complete failure follows.

Safeguards against this type of failure are

(*a*) to raise the walls at least one metre above the highest known, or the design, tide; this applies particularly to estuary walls
(*b*) to make the back slope equal to or flatter than 2½:1
(*c*) to make the top of the wall sufficiently wide so that breaching will not necessarily follow a shallow slip occurring on the landward slope
(*d*) to lay a 75 mm layer of ashes along the top of the wall, this helps to prevent loss of moisture and thus to reduce fissuring.

3.1.3. Back scour

Scouring of the back of the wall, if it is too severe for turf to provide sufficient protection, can generally only be combated by constructing a protective revetment, which is described in Chapter 4. It is understood that in Holland it is common practice to limit overtopping of earthen walls, unprotected on their landward slopes, to 2×10^{-3}m^3/s per metre, but close attention

69

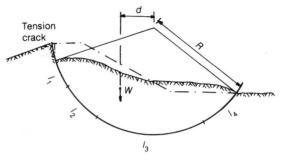

Fig. 26. Diagram showing rotational slip

must be paid to ensuring that shallow slips do not occur (see Section 3.1.2).

In some areas, tipping of suitable waste materials behind the wall can be an effective means of strengthening the wall and preventing at little cost the possibility of breaches occurring.

3.1.4. Rotational slip: slip circle analysis

Failure by rotational slip is a common cause of wall failure during the carrying out of heightening works and Fig. 26 shows the mechanism of a slip of this kind. Such a slip occurred on the landward side of the wall at Scrapsgate, Isle of Sheppey. Fig. 27 shows the heave in the delph ditch and the wall profile before and after failure. It is therefore essential that scheme investigations should include stability analyses to ensure that the proposed improved section will not fail in this way.

Simple slip circle analysis is frequently employed. Referring to Fig. 26, and considering a unit run of wall, the factor of safety is given by $R\Sigma ls/Wd$.

A number of trial circles of different radii and centres are

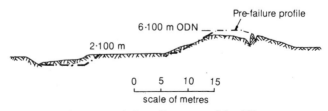

Fig. 27. Failure by rotational slip at Scrapsgate, Isle of Sheppey

70

taken to determine the arc of least stability. The shear strengths at the various depths are found from samples tested in an unconfined compression test machine, the shear strengths of soft clays being approximately equal to half the compression strengths determined directly by the machine. The method assumes that the shear strengths at the various depths will not decrease after construction. The depth of the tension crack is taken as $2s/\alpha$, where α is the density of the bank material.

For walls protecting agricultural land, a factor of safety of 1.2 will normally be found adequate. If at one or two sections along the wall the factor of safety against landward slip is somewhat low, it is usually better to proceed with the work, since if a failure occurs during construction it is not a difficult matter to remedy the failure and strengthen the section. This procedure is generally justified since walls normally strengthen with time (but not always, and this aspect of design is dealt with later).

For walls protecting built-up areas or valuable industrial property, a factor of safety of at least 1.5 is recommended.

In many areas it is found that the saltings in front of a wall are at a higher level than the land protected. In these cases failure by rotational slip landwards on heightening the wall could occur, particularly if there is a delph ditch close to the wall on the landward side. If the factor of safety determined is too low, conditions can usually be improved by filling in the ditch and constructing a berm on the landward side. Similarly where failure is likely on the seaward side, the factor of safety can be improved by weighting the seaward toe of the wall.

As an initial approximation, assuming the shear strength s to be constant at all depths, the maximum height of wall possible with normal side slopes is $(5.5s)/\alpha$, where α is the density of the bank material. Since the shear strength of marsh clays* is often about 1.0 or 1.5 Mg/m^2 and α about 1.6 Mg/m^3, it follows that the height of walls is limited to between 3.5 and 5.2 m above marsh level, unless special (and expensive) works such as berms are provided to increase the factor of safety. The critical wall heights for various clay densities and shear strengths may be read directly from Design Chart O.

* Multiply by g, i.e. 9.81 to convert to kN.

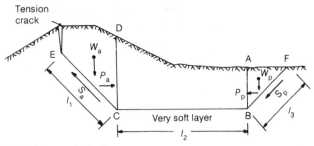

Fig. 28. Wedge analysis diagram

The simple analyses described in this Section are known as φ = 0 analyses and the basis and justification for using this approach in the design of sea walls are given in Section 3.2. Computer programs exist (for example, reference 2) to facilitate the carrying out of the analyses. In difficult circumstances, the more complex approach, taking into account values of the cohesion c, the effective stress p_1 and the angle of internal friction φ (see Section 3.2), is used and examples of this are given for tidal walls in Section 3.8 and for clay cliffs in Section 6.7.

3.1.5. Gravitational slip: wedge analysis

Where the underlying strata are thin layers of soft clay, wedge analysis is preferable to slip circle analysis, but the latter method is more accurate for fairly uniform clay deposits. In the former case, the surface of sliding consists of several sections which do not run smoothly together, so that an error is introduced if the surface is assumed to be an arc of a circle.

Wedge analyses are carried out as follows. Referring to Fig. 28, if P_a is the active disturbing earth force acting on CD, P_p the passive resisting earth force acting on AB and L_2T_2 the shear force acting on BC, then

$$\text{factor of safety} = \frac{P_p + L_2T_2}{P_a}$$

Trial postitions for B and C are taken and wedge analyses carried out until the surface of least factor of safety is determined.

For soft clays, CE and FB may be taken at 45° to the horizontal. With a factor of safety F, if a force diagram is drawn for DCE, it will be seen that

$$P_a = W_a - \sqrt{2}S_a = W_a - \frac{\sqrt{2}L_1 T_1}{F}$$

and similarly

$$P_p = W_p + \sqrt{2}S_p = W_p + \frac{\sqrt{2}L_3 T_3}{F}$$

Whence, for equilibrium

$$W_a - \frac{\sqrt{2}L_1 T_1}{F} = W_p + \frac{\sqrt{2}L_3 T_3}{F} + \frac{T_2 L_2}{F}$$

This derivation was provided by Marsland.

Computer programs that facilitate the carrying out of the analyses exist (see Section 3.8).

3.1.6. Delayed slips

Delayed slips sometimes occur up to nine months or more after construction. The reasons for these are usually complex and in many cases not fully understood. Among the causes listed by Marsland[3] of the Building Research Establishment are re-distribution of pore-water pressure, excessive pore-water pressures resulting from changes in tidal level, and banks built of appreciably stiffer material than the very compressive underlying soil, resulting in differential settlement sufficient to cause extensive cracks to develop especially in the centre of the bank.

Even where failure does not occur, slow settlement of walls is very common where the underlying material is very soft.

3.1.7. Uplift pressures

If a permeable stratum exists under a clay wall, it will be evident that, on high tides, uplift pressures could develop under the wall. These can reduce the stability of the wall by lessening the shear strength of the soil and even by causing the landward toe to heave. One remedy is to provide more weight on the landward side; alternatively to provide relief filter drains near the landward toe to reduce the uplift pressures, or a combination of more weight and relief filter drains.

Details of investigations for and design of a landward weighting berm to counter uplift under extreme conditions are given in Sections 3.7, 3.8 and 3.9.

3.2 SHEARING RESISTANCE, COHESION, EFFECTIVE AND NEUTRAL STRESSES AND ANGLE OF INTERNAL FRICTION

The general relation between shearing resistance s, cohesion c, effective (intergranular) stress p_1 and the angle of internal friction ϕ of soils is given by the equation $s = c + p_1 \tan \phi$.

If the load on the soil at a given level is p per unit area and the pore-water pressure (neutral pressure) is u, then $p_1 = p - u$. Thus it will be seen that as the pore-water pressure increases the shear strength decreases. For clayey soils, the pore-water pressure is usually at a maximum directly after construction and becomes a minimum as the clay consolidates with time.

Pore-water pressures vary with change in the imposed shear stress on clays. If it is assumed that the pore-water pressures developed during shearing are the same both in the test sample and in the ground, then the shear strength results of unconfined compression tests can be taken as the shear strength of the clay in the stability analyses. Investigations on this assumption are known as $\phi = 0$ analyses. Analyses on this basis for the design of most walls built in marshy areas are used because experience shows them to give satisfactory results with the factors of safety quoted in Section 3.1.4. and because of the ease of carrying out unconfined compression tests.

Values of c and ϕ may be ascertained from samples tested in a triaxial compression machine. Analyses taking values of c and ϕ into account are dealt with in Sections 3.8. and 6.7.

3.3 STABILITY OF SILT AND SAND WALLS

Permeable silt and sand walls unprotected by revetments are sometimes used as counterwalls, as second lines of defence some distance landward of the main defences. If breaches occurred in the main walls, the counterwalls would contain the water flowing through the breaches, but would not be subjected to wave action. The strength of these pervious walls deteriorates as the water level rises towards the crest because of the drag exerted by the seeping water.

Simple stability analyses for this type of wall are usually based on the Swedish method of slices. The flow net is plotted (by a method described in detail below) and unit thickness of the wall section is divided into vertical slices above the trial slip circle arc. The total weight of each slice (saturated, if it is below the line of saturation) is resolved at right angles to and tangential to the arc. The former is the normal reaction which, divided by the length of the arc, gives the applied load per unit area p, and the latter the disturbing force F_D.

The average pore-water pressure u acting on the length of arc considered is determined from the net flow, and then, from the equation given in Section 3.2, the shear strength s is obtained. The restoring force F_R is then s times the length of the arc. It therefore follows that the factor of safety is $\Sigma F_R / \Sigma F_D$. In this method, the forces between the slices are usually neglected and generally this errs on the side of safety.

Although some scale effects must occur (since the Weber number cannot be the same for model and prototype), it has been shown that reliable information on seepage can be obtained from hydraulic models of permeable walls, provided certain simple rules are followed. Where the permeabilities of the materials in different zones of the embankment differ, corresponding portions of the model are made of materials which have the same relative permeabilities. With materials coarser than 2 mm the flow is not streamlined. Bearing in mind these conditions, a model is made and from it the line of saturation is determined. Once that is known, the net flow can easily be plotted by the well-known Forchheimer method.[4]

3.4 UNDER-DRAINAGE, AGGREGATE FILTERS AND FILTER MEMBRANES

If the flow lines reach the surface of the back slope of the wall, local failure can occur either in the form of local slumping or local erosion caused by the seeping water carrying the material down the slope. This can be remedied by thickening the bank, or by providing an under-drain filter under the landward toe of the wall to 'draw down' the flow.

To be effective, the particles forming the filter must not be too small, since they must be big enough to provide the drain with a greater permeability than the wall to achieve the required 'draw down'. On the other hand, they must not be too big, otherwise the material of the bank could be drawn into the interstices and thus obstruct the flow. These two conditions can be avoided if the Terzaghi criteria are applied. These are that the 15% size (D_{15}) of the filter (that is, size of sieve through which 15% of the sample passes) is at least four times as large as the D_{15} size of the coarsest wall material sample and not more than four times as large as the 85% size (D_{85}) of the finest wall material sample.

The designer is sometimes faced with the problem of building a revetment to protect permeable material that cannot be drained landward, as in the example just given and in Section 3.5. To prevent the build-up of excessive hydrostatic pressures under the revetment, the practice is to ensure that the revetment is permeable, for example that it is formed of interlocking blocks or riprap, laid on a layer of stone, itself laid on a filter membrane designed to retain the soil but release the water.

Filter membranes are available from a number of manufacturers and are usually made of synthetic fibres, such as polyvinylidene chloride, polypropylene and polyethylene. Membranes made of multifilament yarns are not recommended since they absorb water, causing the individual yarns to swell and thereby reducing the size of the openings.

The object of the stone layer is to provide maximum release of water through the revetment, which would not occur if interlocking blocks were laid directly on the membrane, and in the case of riprap, to distribute the load of the large stones. In addition, the stone must be open enough to permit free flow of water and sufficiently large not to move through the interstices. The thickness of the stone layer varies according to the details of the overlying stone in the case of a riprap apron. As far as interlocking blocks are concerned, this type of design has been used successfully in the USA, for example at Delray Beach, Florida and at Cedarhunt and Benedict, Maryland. A typical thickness for the stone layer (usually consisting of 10–25 mm or 40 mm stone) under the interlocking blocks is 200 mm, which

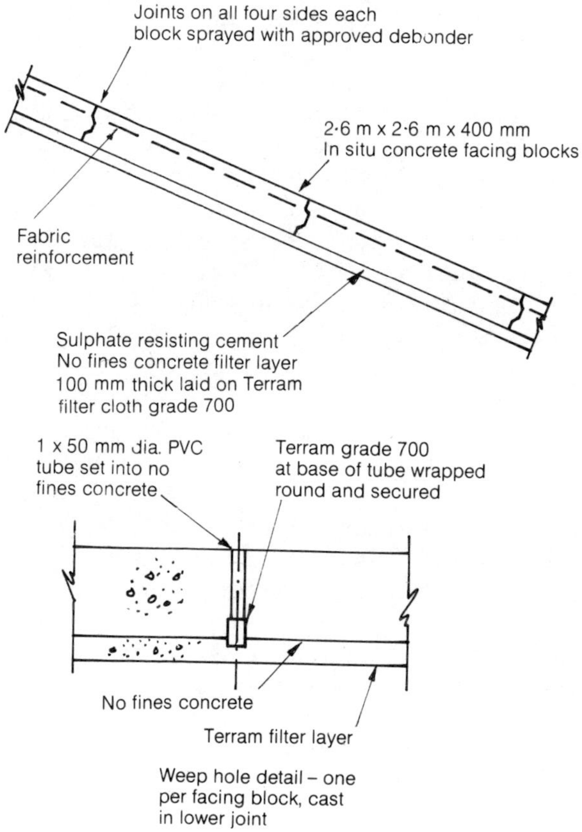

Fig. 29.   Design to reduce hydrostatic pressure under blockwork apron

would appear to be a generous provision. The layer should not be more permeable than is necessary to drain the embankment material, since the more permeable it is, the less is the stability of the interlocking blocks[5] (and see Section 4.12).

The filter membrane is equivalent to a graded aggregate filter. As water passes through it, there is initially a small loss of soil particles, but larger particles build up against it, forming a filter. Design therefore proceeds by determining first the graded aggregate filter characteristics that would otherwise be required, and then selecting from data provided by the membrane manufacturer a suitable equivalent membrane having

77

the same pore-size distribution characteristics.

Where the foundation is of sand, the Delft expression developed for non-woven membranes may be used,[6] that is the membrane should be such that $O_{90}/D_{90} \leqslant 1.8$, where O is the fabric pore size diameter, D the sand particle size diameter and 90 represents 90% of all sand particles or pores smaller than this size. Makers of filter membranes provide pore size distribution curves from which a suitable membrane may then be chosen.

It is sometimes necessary to prevent the building up of excessive uplift pressures, due to seepage from the landward side, under an impermeable apron. Fig. 29 shows how this was achieved on a length of the Sheerness Wall, Isle of Sheppey, where seepage from a moat on the landward side of the wall had to be dealt with. It will be seen that the filter layer drains seaward through holes in the apron comprising plastic tubes containing nylon filters. The no-fines concrete filter layer comprised sulphate resisting cement, coarse aggregate 20 mm single size to Table 1, BS 882;[7] of grade 20 N/mm².

As the surface of the water recedes prior to the wave breaking on the apron, the water on the apron can be at a lower level than still water level, consequently the water in the underlying filter layer, at approximately still water level (but reducing in the case of interlocking blocks with flow through the joints) will exert an uplift on the underside of the apron. If the apron is flexible, this could raise it slightly, creating a temporary void that would reduce this pressure, provided the filter layer is not highly permeable. Also, the shear strength of the apron (or of its joints if interlocking) would spread the load to surrounding parts of the apron. It is important to ensure that this is not accompanied by permanent deformation of the filter layer creating permanent voids under the apron and thereby weakening the apron. One possible way of meeting this requirement is to use no-fines concrete made with sulphate-resisting cement for the filter layer, as on the length of the Sheerness Wall seaward of the moat.

3.5   USE OF SAND IN SEA WALLS

There is a great deal of sand on the coasts of Holland and Germany and consequently in those areas sand is a much used

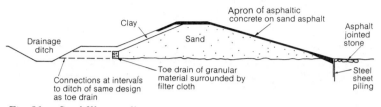

Fig. 30.   Sand fill sea wall

material in sea wall construction. Fig. 30 is a cross-section of a sea wall of this kind where heavy wave action will not occur. The basis of the design is to provide a seaward sheet piling cut-off wall, an impermeable seaward face of asphaltic concrete laid on sand asphalt, clay on the landward face and a sand core together with adequate under-drainage consisting in present-day design of granular material surrounded by a suitable filter membrane (see Section 3.4).

The precise mixes for the asphaltic concrete and sand asphalt will depend on the temperature range, the slope of the apron, its aspect (whether facing north or south) and other site circumstances. Specialist knowledge is required here and the expert advice of the petroleum companies that supply bitumen should be sought. For example, on the island of Goeree-Overflakkee, Holland, with a seaward slope of 3½:1, the sand asphalt base course, varying in thickness from 400 mm at the toe to 100 mm on the crest, comprised (by weight) 84% fine sand, 8% filler, and 8% bitumen 50/60. The asphaltic concrete, 100 mm thick, comprised by weight 43% chippings of 2–12 mm, 42% sand of 0–2 mm, 8% filler, and 7% bitumen 50/60. A tack coat of bitumen 280/320 was used between the two layers and to seal the top course, at 1.5 kg/m^2; crushed gravels of 3–5 mm applied hot was used as cover.

It would appear that determination of the thickness of the seaward apron required mainly proceeds on the basis of selecting a thickness comparable to that of similar existing aprons which experience has shown have satisfactorily withstood similar conditions. Pending the securing of such information, an initial tentative approach could be to use the method set out for monolithic stone aprons given in Section 4.12, making full allowance for the lower specific weights and shear strengths of the bituminous materials.

It will be appreciated that where heavy wave action is expected, Dutch practice is to provide a stone, usually asphalt-jointed, apron, on a clay layer overlying the sand, and in that case the design method for deciding the thickness is that set out in detail in Section 4.12. Details of mixes for asphalt joints are given in Sections 4.10 and 4.18.

Another application of sand is in the improvement of existing clay estuary walls on saltings where circumstances are such that it is not desirable to construct the improvement on the landward side.

The wall is raised in sand on the seaward side, with a clay cut-off connecting to the existing clay wall, a stone (or stone-protected shingle/sand) seaward weighting berm if this is required on soil mechanics grounds. The seaward face of the wall is protected by riprap designed in accordance with Section 4.25, if considerable settlement is expected.

To prevent leaching of the sand and to drain the sand adequately, a filter membrane (see Section 3.4) is placed on the sand and under the stone layer on which the riprap is placed (see Sections 3.4 and 4.25).

The use of sand in landward weighting berms is explained in Section 3.6.

3.6 WEIGHTING BERMS IN SEA DEFENCE WORKS

There are four main reasons for using the concept of bermed construction.

These are

(a) to stabilise a slope by weighting the toe of possible slip circles (see Fig. 31)

(b) to increase the length of possible slip planes, especially non-circular slips (see Fig. 31), and where uplift problems occur (see Fig. 34)

(c) to improve the strength of the foundation soils when used with a phased construction method

(d) to counteract, where applicable, the flotation effects of uplift pressures from underlying permeable strata (see Fig. 34).

It will be noticed that all the examples in this Section are il-

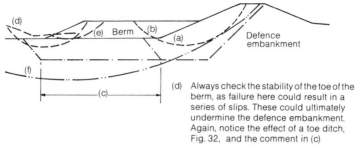

(a) Original possible slip circle stabilized

(b) Note: always check that a rear face circular slip up through the berm cannot occur

(c) Lengthened slip plane in considering a non-circular slip, for example a wedge type failure, as illustrated in this case. Care needs also to be taken of hinterland features, for example ditches, see Fig. 32.

(d) Always check the stability of the toe of the berm, as failure here could result in a series of slips. These could ultimately undermine the defence embankment. Again, notice the effect of a toe ditch, Fig. 32, and the comment in (c)

(e) The first of a series of secondary slips as referred to in (d) above

(f) Possible large radius circular slip resulting in a total defence failure. Note: experience has proved that on alluvial clayey soils. failure planes are unlikely to pass more than 7m below the general ground level, and such failures usually follow the shallower, weaker soils and become non-circular.

Fig. 31. Forms of wall failure

lustrated by the examination of possible landward slips. It should be realised, however, that a failure of an embankment sea- or riverward is also possible. Further, owing to the ensuing problems of reinstatement of defences, this form of failure would probably be the more serious. Notes on seaward stability and toe loading will be found later in this Section.

Other than drawing attention in Figs. 31 and 32 to the variety and inter-relation of the various slip failure mechanisms, it is not proposed to cover (*a*) and (*b*) in greater detail. The analysis of failures is covered generally in Sections 3.1.4 and 3.1.5, and in depth in most soil mechanics books.

The use of berms to improve the strength characteristics of soft clay and laminated clay soils is a very important application, as relatively small strength gains (for example $5kN/m^2$) are significant when considering soft soils. Adequate time must be allowed between the construction of the berm and the raising of the embankment, although, if adequate factors of safety are possible, subsequent stages may be progressed with only partial consolidation having occurred. The consolidation period can be broadly estimated from site investigation works and testing, and from previous experience at the same location. Hydraulic piezometer profiles should be installed in the clays

81

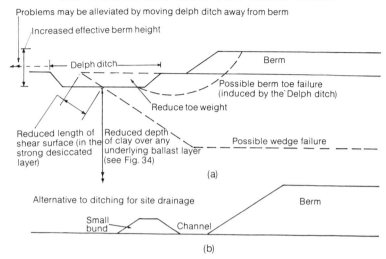

Fig. 32. Effect of excavation on berm stability

under the berm to observe the consolidation, by means of recording the decay in excess pore-water pressures.

The consolidation effects on soil strength should be confirmed by further laboratory testing of the foundation soils. The higher the berm is, the more efficient it will be in producing the required consolidation. Edge or toe stability will limit the height of berm which can be raised. The berm serves another useful purpose in phased construction in reducing the total and differential settlements which will have to be accommodated by the final embankment.

It is worth noting at this juncture that should very weak foundation conditions occur, limited room for a berm be available and/or a very low risk of failure be required, then a defence structure could be erected on the berm instead of on earth embankment. A further advantage of a part structural solution is that a lower defence level may be used, as no allowance need be made for soil desiccation (see Section 3.1.2). It is essential for such a structure to have an adequate cut-off into the berm, or where applicable into the foundation strata, to seal off seepage.

The effect of a berm is to load the clay under the berm and thus increase the pore pressures. These pore pressures are termed 'excess pore-water pressures', that is, above hydrostatic. To effect consolidation and soil strength improvement, it is necessary that these excess pressures be dissipated. The natural preferred dissipation of the soil will probably be horizontal. If, however, the vertical drainage distance is much smaller than the horizontal distance, then the drainage of water could be predominantly vertical. To assist this, drainage berms are often constructed in sand or ballast, and if of clay construction they incorporate a ballast filter layer between the natural ground level and the clay fill. It may be necessary to use a filter cloth under the ballast to prevent contamination by fine particles being washed in by the rising water. Consolidation rates may be further improved by using vertical drains, such as sandwicks or paper/plastic laminate drains to tap off the horizontally drained water in the subsoils. Indeed such work may be essential in laminated soils to stop high pore-water pressures travelling from under the berm, through the permeable layers, to the unloaded toe. This would cause, on a smaller scale, problems such as covered in Section 3.1.7. and illustrated later in this Section, and by Parry.[8]

When considering bermed construction riverwards, several factors must be taken into account. First, many naturally existing berms occur, either in the form of earlier defence works, or as saltings. Also the slope of the shore is usually shallow, but care must be taken in locating sudden changes in river profile, for example, dredged channels or inflowing rivers or creeks which cut through the foreshore.

A berm may be formed on the foreshore, following its natural line or slope. This type of berm is called toe loading. Special care must be taken in planning work of this type, and in the choosing of a material which will not be eroded or displaced by water action. The design must also examine the risk of further material being deposited on the works owing to sedimentation and/or the restricting of littoral drift. The design methods and checks for these works are the same as for the landward berms, with due note of the above remarks. Usually soil data riverward of the defence line are not as complete and as thorough as data on and landward of it. Further, as already noted, the cost and difficulty of replacing a riverward-failed defence is greater than for a landward one. For these two reasons a higher factor

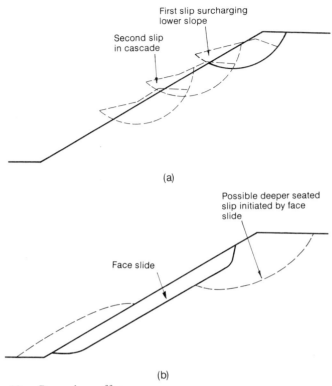

First slip surcharging
lower slope

Second slip
in cascade

(a)

Possible deeper seated
slip initiated by face
slide

Face slide

(b)

Fig. 33.   Draw-down effects

of safety should be used in designing the river or seaward side
of defence works.

A problem peculiar to the riverward side of the defences is
draw down. On a tidal defence this usually results in a very
shallow form of failure, either as in Fig. 33 (a), a cascade of slip
circles, or as in Fig. 33(b), a long shallow face slide. While not
necessarily serious in themselves, these types of failure could
easily precipitate failures of a more serious nature. They also
necessitate comparatively expensive seaward restabilising and
re-facing. The effects of such cascade failures are minimised by
ensuring that the crest of the defence embankment is adequately wide, say 3.0 m minimum. The occurrence of such
draw-down failure can be reduced by ensuring that the permeability of the surface layers increases with nearness to the

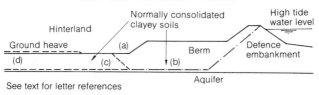

Fig. 34. Wedge-type failure with uplift

surface and also by providing a high permeability face protection. Alternatively, the surface may be sealed to prevent water penetration. Careful attention must therefore be paid to the front face stability.

One final factor remains in considering the general design of berms. This is the elimination of seepage and the risk of 'piping', and to this end, with permeable material in the bund, a cut-off would be required. In constructing a cut-off it may be necessary to excavate through the surface strata and place a clay core onto intact foundation clay or rock.

When considering the special case of a wedge-type failure in normally consolidated soils, for example, marsh clay, which overlies an aquifer under tidally responsive artesian pressures, then two special failure cases are possible (see Fig. 34).

(i) The uplift pressures below (a) exceed the downward loading from the soils and the soil is effectively blown out, destroying the stabilising effect of the wedge of soil at the toe of the berm. If immediate failure of the defence does not occur, then rapid progressive failure is possible from a circular slip of the berm edge at (a). This would thus start a cascade of similar slips which could ultimately undermine the landward face of the defence embankment.

(ii) The effective stress due to increased pore-water pressures at (b) and (c) is reduced to a very low value. This, in turn, for a normally consolidated soil, will reduce the shear strength to nearly zero. A wedge failure then occurs. Alternatively, instead of throwing upwards a wedge of soil at (a) the failure continues horizontally through (c). The soil being soft, will squeeze up at (c) and (d) giving very small and probably imperceptible increases in ground level. Hence a slip could occur without visible warning or effect at the toe of the defence works.

85

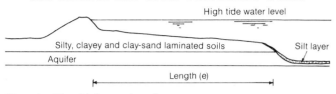

Fig. 35.   Aquifer–tidal water interface

From studies made by computer analysis and field observation there is a case for proposing a special relationship which occurs at an aquifer/tidal water interface.

The tide acts as a loading on the soils under the foreshore which results in an increase in pore pressures over this length (length (e) in Fig. 35) in the clayey and silty soils of the foreshore. This hydraulic pressure is less than the potential of the tide-water head. These pore-pressure rises are transmitted as a pressure surge which travels up the aquifer layer in a landward direction, and hence the tidal response of the aquifer. Because the water pressure on the riverward side of the silt layer is still greater than the pore-water pressure in the aquifer, the silts are compacted into a tight and relatively impermeable layer. Thus little flow actually migrates across this silt boundary.

At low tide any residual pressure in the aquifer, for example, from ground water flow, blows through the silt layer. This is facilitated by the pressure in the aquifer being greater than the tide-water head. Hence, by means of this one-way valve effect of the silt layer, the aquifer can drain into the river even though the mean water head in the aquifer may be lower than mean tide level.

One method of solving the problems resulting from high pressures in an underlying aquifer is to provide pressure relief. This may be in the form of bores which are allowed overflow naturally into a drainage system, or of well points which are pumped when the pressures in the aquifer reach dangerous levels. Two very important aspects of these types of remedial work are the frequency and the transverse locations of the bores, or well points, to ensure protection to the berm toe and the wall's hinterland. Where uncertainties exist, there is a strong case for including pressure relief in the design.

The only method of assessing the effects of the tide levels on the pore-water pressure in an aquifer is by long time scale reading sets. Each set should record tide level and groundwater head, and should cover a substantial part of a tidal cycle, including the maximum water head reading in the aquifer. From these results for different tide levels an approximate design case response can be extrapolated (see also Section 3.7). Useful references on weighting berms are two reports from the Building Research Establishment.[1,9]

3.7   SITE INVESTIGATION AND INSTRUMENTATION

It is proposed to divide this Section into two parts.

(a) Site investigation is the process of deriving information about the soils and geology, and in some cases the topography, of a proposed site.

(b) Instrumentation is used to observe the performance and reaction of the soils due to some disturbing influence. This is, in the case of sea and river defences, usually the result of creating or raising a defence embankment and/or structure. Instrumentation works are used sometimes to observe natural 'disturbing influences' (for example, tide rise and fall), and their effect on the soil strata.

3.7.1. Site investigation

It is not within the scope of this book to explain fully all the facets of site investigation, but rather to give a few guides on the approach to this type of work, together with comments about the most usual sources of error. Site investigations should always be undertaken with the assistance of competent specialists.

First, adequate monies must be put aside for this work, say between 2½ and 4% of the project value for earthworks. Second, the work must be given clear objectives as to the information required by the design teams. Third, an organised approach must be made towards obtaining that information, considering also cost and programme limitations. Finally, careful and meticulous reporting must be undertaken on the observations made and results obtained. This phase includes

87

the correlation of data from all results into usable formats. Throughout the site investigation, all work must be of the highest technical standard realistically attainable, if meaningful results are to be obtained.

The achieving of the first and second targets are self-explanatory and essential. The second and third targets may be usefully examined in the light of earlier work in the area and by reference to geological maps and area descriptive notes. The third target is best achieved by phasing of the work in the following way.

Phase 1. An initial run of boreholes is made to provide a clear outline of soil types and stratification. These holes should generally be about 200–300 m apart. This run of boreholes should be solely used for slicing and the describing of the soils, with extensive index testing and an almost negligible amount of tri-axial, shearbox, permeability or consolidation testing. Also, very little instrumentation should be installed during this phase. It is useful at this stage to reference the different soil types (see Table 3.1 for an example) and to define clearly the descriptive terms to be used.

Phase 2. Having identified the soil types, their occurrence, and their importance to the final works, a testing schedule for each one should be produced. The testing selected should examine the relevant properties to the appropriate degree, depending on how critical they are to the final design work. A schedule of boreholes, sampling and instrument installation should also be made at this stage. Note that work should be concentrated on clearly discernible soil types (for example, silty sands, laminated clays) to facilitate later data correlation.

Phase 3. From Phase 2 certain soils or problems will show up as requiring further investigation. This may mean sub-dividing soil types, expanding existing test and/or instrumentation schedules, or expanding the area of work. It may also necessitate the introducing of sophisticated and expensive sampling, testing and instrumentation techniques within a limited band or area of operation. Adequate financial provision and contractual flexibility must be incorporated into the site investigation programme and contractual arrangements to allow for this phase of work.

It should be noted that with programme restrictions more

Table 3.1 Example of a standardised description of samples (as used by the Southern Water Authority on the Thames Tidal Flood Defences Scheme)

All samples were described and photographed in accordance with the specification. Special care was taken to note any layering, varving or laminations found in the samples. As the soil conditions varied greatly this simplified classification system was used to group each sample into one of seven major soil types, with sub-type if appropriate.

Soil type	Description	Sub-type (suffix)	Description
Type 1	CLAY, with suffixes a, d, o and s (see below)	a	With some/frequent/abundant pockets and/or laminations of peat and/or plant remains
Type 2	PEAT (see below)		
Type 3	Silty SAND or sandy SILT, with suffixes a and o, possibly including small amounts of clay or peat lenses and occasional laminations	c	Applicable to laminated materials, where laminations are either inclined, infrequent, discontinuous or contorted, or where the secondary material occurs predominantly in pockets and/or lenses
Type 4	Clayey SILT or clayey SAND, possibly including small amounts of clay or peat lenses and occasional laminations	d	Implies desiccated material
Type 5	SAND or SILT with CLAY laminations, with suffixes a and o	o	Implies organic material other than peat as the basic constituents of the main soil type; it shall exclude those soils where the organic material is substantially in pockets, laminations and inclusions
Type 5p	SAND or SILT with CLAY partings		
Type 6	CLAY with SAND laminations, with suffixes a, c, d, o and s	s	Where some/frequent/abundant pre-existing shear planes or listric surfaces are found
Type 7	GRAVEL		

The suffixes shown with the material types are those that are commonly used, for example, 6c, 6co. Other suffixes may be applied if necessary, for example, 5p. Note that more than one suffix may be used to define a sub-type. PEAT to be described as being of either fibrous, amorphous or of the hard elastic type, and to be clearly differentiated from decayed individual plant remains and organic soils where appropriate.

89

than one phase will probably be in progress at any one time.

The fourth and final target is again self-explanatory. The insistence on detailed and thorough borehole logging cannot be over-emphasised. These logs can usefully be backed-up by a large scale photography operation, to produce, say, 35 mm colour slides for the purpose of accurately recording each sample in detail. Care should be taken in logging and reporting to ensure consistency in the descriptions and terminology used. It should be noted that engineers' standard terms should be used and not those of geologists, which can, in some cases, give a totally opposite meaning. Adequate provision should be made for the considerable amount of manpower and time that the reporting work entails.

Some observations on specific factors will next be made, but these will not be an exhaustive catalogue of methods or possible difficulties in site investigation. There can be no substitute for the involvement of experienced personnel in this field.

The first important element for consideration is obtaining good samples. For example, in the alluvial soils normally associated with estuarine and marsh conditions, piston samples[10] should always be used in preference to U100 or other percussive method. The U100 or similar should only be used if the piston sample is constantly refused, for example, by a ballast layer. Other information on soil sampling is given by Terzaghi and Peck.[11] Undisturbed samples should be taken continuously in the Phase 1 boreholes for descriptive purposes, as bulk samples can be totally misleading if relied upon to observe substantial lengths of bore. Even in ballasts, for example, the washing out of fines by bulk sampling would lead to a totally false estimation of the permeability of the ballast.

The second point to examine is ensuring the relevance of the testing proposed. Two examples are taken to illustrate this.

Example 1. If very substantial elements of the failure are anticipated to be horizontal, then 'preferred orientation' testing must be undertaken. This is where the soil is induced to fail along a plane in the specimen which would have been horizontal in the ground (that is, total reliance should not be placed on a conventional tri-axial and shearbox testing).

Example 2. If the horizontal permeability of a silt, clay, laminated clay or similar soil is required to examine consolidation problems, then two concepts must be considered. First, field permeability testing is the appropriate test for this parameter, but the testing must avoid the hydraulic fracture of the soil, which would cause totally erroneous test results. The test should therefore be undertaken using negative head (that is, below water table) techniques which are not commonly used. The type of equipment necessary for this type of work is manufactured by Jaybury Ltd of East Peckham (near Maidstone), Kent. It is very important that any Casagrande piezometer tip used for this type of testing shall not have been subject to any positive water head at any prior time.

A third aspects refers back to the need to ensure that initial aims and total objectives of the investigation are being met. For example, how sensitive is the proposed design to the variations within a single parameter coming from the testing? Another case would be where instrumentation and observation of a phenomenon have been used and results recorded. These results could then be amplified from empirical observations, by, say, computer modelling, to produce usable design data. The value of universities in this work should not be ignored as they are sources of knowledge and experience, with a substantial capability for undertaking very specialised testing.

3.7.2. Instrumentation

The use of instrumentation, other than as a component of site investigation work, is to monitor construction in progress, and to establish its effect on the soils under, around and/or incorporated into the works. This monitoring enables the site investigation, the design assumptions and calculations, and the construction methods to be examined as construction work progresses.

The installation of instruments is specialised, and the decisions on their frequency and location are best left to expert personnel. It is considered, however, that an outline of some instruments and their functions would be useful, although more detailed data would be available from manufacturers/suppliers, for example Soil Instruments Ltd of Uckfield, East Sussex. The outline information is summarised in tabular form as follows:

Table 3.2   Piezometers: these instruments measure the head or pressure of the groundwater at the tip (bottom) of the instrument

Table 3.3   Ground movement instruments

Table 3.4   Ground pressure instruments: these instruments measure the pressure in a particular plane in the ground.

(See also Section 6.7.)

Three British Standards Institution publications are relevant to this type of work. They are

BS 1377:1975   Methods of test for soils for civil engineering purposes.

BS 5573:1978   (formerly CP 2011: 1969) Safety precautions in the construction of large diameter boreholes for piling and other purposes.

BS   590:1981   (formerly CP 2001: 2957) Code of practice for site investigations.

The use of the first and third publications is obvious. The second publication is important where a confined space exists, for example, gaugehouses, manholes and deep trial pits. Deep trial pits must also be adequately shored for the protection of the people working in them.

3.8   COMPUTER-AIDED DESIGN AND ANALYSIS

The large scale use of computers in design and data analysis is increasing, but with a vast and evolving range of machines, methods and computer programming languages, it can be a confusing subject. It is not in the realm of this book to list fully and explain the potentials of each option in the field, but rather to advise on a general approach pattern. As an example the program used in the design of earthworks for the Thames Tidal Flood Defences by the Kent River and Water Division of the Southern Water Authority is explained in outline at the end of this Section.

The most important capability of a computer is its ability to handle vast quantities of calculations. Indeed the basic process is to break complex problems down into lengthy series of basi-

Table 3.2. Piezometers

Instrument	Description	Comments
Casagrande (stand-pipe) piezometer	Small bore vertical pipe with porous tip at bottom. Water level is read by dipping	Cheap. Should be installed in a sand cell at bottom of bore. Slow to respond in low permeability soils due to large water flows required to alter water levels in standpipe. Used for negative head permeability test using Jaybury equipment
Hydraulic (twin lead) piezometer	Measures pore-water pressure at a ceramic tip via a hydraulic (de-aired water) connection	Expensive due to requirement for gauge house or complex mobile reading unit (say specially equipped Land Rover). Twin leads required to flush marsh gases (for example, methane and hydrogen sulphide) from tip and leads which would affect readings
Pneumatic piezometer	Measures pore-water pressure at a ceramic tip via a transducer and a pneumatic or hydraulic (oil) connection	Simpler readout arrangement than a hydraulic piezometer. Greater separation between tip and readout is possible than with hydraulic piezometers. Unsuitable for long term negative pore-water pressures or where gases occur (as in marsh clays)
Acoustic piezometer	Measures pore-water pressure at a ceramic tip via an electronic transducer and cable connection	Accurate and stable for long term observation. Very remote (1000m+) readout points possible. Fast response due to low actuating volume changes. Unsuitable for long term negative pore-water pressures or where gases occur (as in marsh clays)

NOTES   (*a*) Piezometers must be carefully grouted in to stop flows up and down borehole, and to avoid the grouting up (making impermeable) of sand cells and tips

        (*b*) All instruments must be adequately protected, where at or near the surface, from weather (including frost), construction traffic and machinery, theft and vandalism

93

Table 3.3(a). Ground movement instruments: horizontal movements

Instrument	Description	Comments
Inclinometer	Measures by means of a 'torpedo' and portable readout the inclination of consecutive lengths of a continuous, nominally vertical tube, inserted and grouted into a borehole. The base of the tube is in a nominally 'fixed' layer.	Ground movements calculated by summation of distance × inclination products from base upwards More accurate to log inclinations and subsequently compute deflections than to log summated deflections directly Critical to the design of bentonite/cement grout used
Inverted pendulum	Pendulum pivot point is grouted into the lower 'fixed' layer, and the pendulum wire is tensioned by a float system Hence wire pendulum arm is kept vertical	More expensive than inclinometer and therefore cannot be used as prolifically Very accurate Can be used as a fixed point for other survey work
Portable clinometer and extensometer	Studs are fixed close together into the ground or structure, and the relative distance and angle of slope between the same observed, for change, indicating relative movements	Simple and reliable Very adaptable Very limited base length available for observation (thus it is limited to crack and relative local distortion observations)

94

Table 3.3 (b). Ground movement instruments : vertical movements

Instrument	Description	Comments
Deep datum	Consists of an outer casing allowing the free vertical movement of an inner rod. Inner rod is grouted into a lower 'fixed' stratum	Simple. Necessary for levelling in piezometer water-head reference levels, and all other vertical movement instruments not referenced to lower 'fixed' stratum. Bench-mark for other survey work
Settlement plate	A plate laid at the commencement of fill with a vertical pole attached. Settlement logged by level surveying of the pole head	Simple. Vertical rod susceptible to damage during construction works
Hydrostatic profile gauge	A probe is passed through a nominally horizontal tube, and the deflection of the tube is determined on a portable readout via a fluid pressure/electrical transducer	Simple and reliable. Complete profile across a section can be logged. Limitations exist on profile length, and the range and accuracy possible. Can be adapted to additionally observe horizontal ground movements
Magnetic probe extensometer	Consists of a compressible, nominally vertical inner tube between magnet rings fixed into the ground at different points. The level of the magnet rings is determined by reed switch probe, with reference to a bottom magnet ring cast into a nominally 'fixed' lower stratum. Probe access via hollow tube	Simple to use, reliable and accurate, but requires experience to install well. Critical to the design of bentonite/cement grout used to grout the compressible tube into bore-hole. As described by Marsland and Quarterman, *Geotéchnique*, **24** (3), 429–433
Pneumatic settlement cell	A sealed cell is installed at the point to be logged. Movement is monitored by pressure change in the cell, referenced to a datum point by a fluid (mercury) connection. Cell readout connection is pneumatic	Reliable and simple to read and install, also vertical access is not necessarily required. Unaffected by temperature or lateral ground movements. Large range, but limited precision (± 10 mm), also limited to logging only one point per cell used. Common portable readout unit with pneumatic piezometers

95

Table 3.4. Ground pressure instruments

Instrument	Description	Comments
Acoustic pressure cells	Ground pressure acting perpendicular to the face of a thin, flat hydraulic jack actuates a hydraulic pressure transducer. Transducer/ readout connection is by cable	Accurate, and stable for long-term observation. Remote (1000 m +) readout points possible. Very remote (1000 m + readout points possible). Common portable readout unit with acoustic piezo-meters
Pneumatic/hydraulic pressure cells	Similar to above except that connection is via a non-electrical transducer and a pneumatic or hydraulic (oil) connection	Simple and, being hydro/mechanical, avoids complex electronics (and damp problems). Cells sensitive to temperature change, and therefore unsuitable where large temperature ranges occur. Common portable readout unit with pneumatic piezo-meters

cally simple mathematical operations. This has two benefits to the design engineer. First, more items can be considered as independent variables, and fewer assumptions need be made with reference to simplifying the handling of numbers to manageable proportions. This means that the design, and the materials or soils involved, can be more accurately modelled. Second, the engineer can consider many more design options in a given time span. This latter capability has an important side effect, in that trials of the favoured design can be undertaken with slightly amended parameters. Thus the design's susceptibility to the quality of data and its sensitivity to any specific variable can be examined, and, with engineering judgment, parameter or design detail alterations can be made to reduce cost and/or risk of the final works.

To return to the modelling of soils, the computer has another major role. This is in the realm of converting raw test data into a form usable by a design engineer. To this end many different formats of correlation can be swiftly and thoroughly examined. One important source of data is the back analysis of failures. This is especially useful when expediting emergency repair or remedial works, when the time is not available for the undertaking of a detailed and thorough soils investigation.

It is important here to recognise what a computer cannot do, which is the production of a result of greater accuracy than that of the data supplied. For example, half guessed parameters from a few rushed tests will give a design result no better, and probably worse, than a competent and experienced engineer could have produced with the aid of a few simple hand calculations. The scope therefore for this kind of sophisticated design tool is where substantial quantities of good quality data are available, and sound economic and design quality benefits are the possible rewards of careful and thorough analysis. The word 'tool' was used purposely as this is what a computer system should be to an engineer.

The computer is operated by means of software (note that conversely hardware is the colloquial term for the computer and its ancillary equipment). This software divides into two categories, the first being the operating systems which are individual to each make of computer equipment, and the second being the programs.

97

The operating systems, as their name implies, work the internals of the computer machinery. For the engineer there are two operational options. First there is 'batch' operation, where the machine takes the whole problem, considers it at its own convenience and returns a block of answers. Second there is 'time-sharing' operation, where the machine looks at a whole series of problems apparently concurrently by dedicating a very small time slice ($\ll 1s$) to each problem in turn. This type of system permits 'interactive' programes to be run, where the engineers at different terminals are in 'conversation' with the computer. This is a better form of use for the design engineer who is looking at different cases to optimise a design, because he can change data and/or design options, and receive an immediate result from the computer. Many machines that will operate on an interactive basis utilise spare computer time by running a secondary batch handling facility. It remains to state that while the batch operation is more efficient in the use of the computer, the interactive operation is a vastly more effective design method in terms of engineer time.

The second category of software is the range of programs available to consider and solve specific problems. These are usually written in a standardised computer language, so that they may be transported from a machine of one manufacture or type to another of different manufacture or type. The programs lay out in step-by-step form the actions and calculations necessary to solve the specific problems, for example, the factor of safety for a circular slip. To evaluate the usefulness of a program it is important to know the design method and assumptions on which it is based, and any limitations there may be as to its use.

To the engineer there are three basic options available for access to computer capacity. The viability of each option depends on the combined expertise of the engineers working on a problem and the economics of the costs arising. The first option is to use a bureau which will offer a range of programs running on their own computers. Access to the computer will be either by mail or by telephone line link via a terminal. Most bureaux will also provide the facility of computer power for the developing and running of a customer's own program, but extensive use of such a facility is not really economic, a problem which is compounded in the UK by high telecommunications costs.

The second option is to lease already written and proven programs to run on an internally or preferentially available computer facility. With this option one is often limited by the computer service available to batch operation. A well-known source of available engineering programs is Genesys Ltd of Loughborough, who also operate limited bureau facilities from this location. Examples of the programs available with Genesys include circular and non-circular slip analysis for slope stability, retaining wall design and sheet pile design.

The final option is the use of dedicated in-house computer facilities with substantial provisions for the writing and development of programs.

As an example of computer-aided design it is proposed to examine briefly the use of SRH3 in the analysing of the earthwork defences along the North Kent Bank of the River Thames.

This program (SRH3) operates on an interactive basis, and undertakes both the circular and the non-circular slip analysis of slopes, whether of constant grade or of bermed construction. To handle the problems of partial consolidation it can consider concurrently hydrostatic and non-hydrostatic pore-water pressure distributions. Further, to use fully the concept of the C_u/p_1 parameter, it differentiates between long term and recent loadings, and analyses their different effects on the slow and on the rapid draining soils. This is a specialised program for a specific problem, which also has the potential of development for other applications. The abilities of this program to handle sophisticated soil modelling, and to consider special cases, for example, partial consolidation, were the prime reasons for its original development. Data were, where necessary, derived from other programs, for example, the pore-water pressure distributions in a partial consolidation case were obtained using the HECB program SETTLE.

It is always important when using complex programs of this sort to ensure that the input data quality warrants the use and cost of computer analysis. If good data sources are available then the savings on permanent works from better standards of design could well prove to be in the order of 20%, which

99

justifies the costs involved. This order of saving was achieved over substantial elements of the Thames Tidal Flood Defences Scheme constructed along the Kent river shore.

It is relevant here to explain the need for and the reasoning behind the C_u/p_1 parameter. When considering failure in clayey or laminated clay soils, it is difficult to determine the pore-water pressures at failure, and hence the term p_1 in the formula $s = c + p_1 \tan \phi$ (see Section 3.2). It is also essential to recognise in normally consolidated soils (such as, North Kent Marsh Clays), that soil strength varies with overburden and pore-pressure (that is, with p_1). The purpose of the parameter C_u/p_1 is to enable the soil strength under a given set of factors to be examined with reference to effective stresses (that is, p_1), and to convert these data into an undrained apparent cohesion for use in total stress analyses. Total stress analyses are simpler to undertake and avoid the very difficult and often erroneous estimations of pore pressures at failure. The expression for the strength of the soil would now read

$$C_u = C_o + p_1 \ (C_u/p_1 \text{ ratio})$$

where C_u is the undrained apparent cohesion; C_o is the intercept on the C_u/p_1 plot where $p_1 = 0$ (for a specific soil at a specific location this is a constant), and (C_u/p_1 ratio) is the relationship between C_u and p_1 derived by soil testing. This is a constant for a specific soil with a specific stress history within a given stress band. For normally consolidated soils $C_o = 0$. For heavily overconsolidated soils the C_o term is dominant over a reasonable depth of soil, and therefore, the C_u/p_1 term is usually neglected. It can be shown that the two expressions for soil strength are related, and the similarity of form can be observed.

It is essential that in analysing test results and in design p_1 (effective over-burden stress) must be calculated taking into account the effects of nearby embankments and structures, the history of the loading, and the hydraulic factors of water flow and non-hydrostatic pore-water pressure distribution. The C_u/p_1 ratio is determined from a series of undrained and consolidated undrained tri-axial tests on undisturbed samples.

An advantage of this parameter is that complex ground conditions can be easily modelled, as shown, for example, in a

100

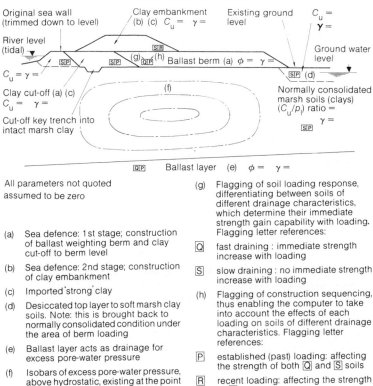

Fig. 36. Typical Thames tidal flood defences (North Kent); sea wall section

typical stability analysis involving a partial consolidation case (as in Fig. 36 which shows a typical Thames Tidal Flood Defences sea wall section).

Further, the value of the parameter may be estimated from Atterberg Limit results. An explanation of the relationship between C_u and p_1 is given by Terzaghi and Peck.[11]

General considerations

3.9 ORIGINAL WAVERLEY COMMITTEE RECOMMENDATIONS

As a result of the east coast flooding in 1953, a Departmental Committee, known as the Waverley Committee after its chairman was set up to examine the causes of the flooding and to make such recommendations as they thought necessary.[12]

The Committee recommended that where residential and industrial areas or large areas of valuable agricultural land would be affected, the standard of protection should be sufficient to withstand the conditions occurring on 31 Jan./1 Feb. 1953. Elsewhere, the standard should be that which would have been thought adequate to withstand the worst known conditions prior to 1953.

In some circumstances, where property of exceptional value has to be protected, or for other exceptional reasons, higher standards than the foregoing could be applied, and similarly where the value of the area to be protected is considerably below the general average, lower standards might be appropriate. In the case of a standard higher than the 1953 standard, those requiring it would be expected to pay for it themselves.

These recommendations were made in conjunction with the Committee's proposal that a flood warning system should be organised. This was done and the system is known as the Storm Tide Warning Service.

In 1978, the Flood Protection Research Committee under the chairmanship of Sir Angus Paton were asked to review the Waverley Committee recommendations and a Working Group was set up to do this under the chairmanship of Gordon Cole. Their conclusion was that only the minimum amendments were necessary and these related solely to the standards, no changes were made to the other recommendations such as those on access, counterwalls and so on, which are dealt with later in this chapter.

3.10   REVISION OF WAVERLEY STANDARDS OF PROTECTION

Basically the revisions are as follows.

(*a*) Where the original recommendations referred to the 1953 conditions, the reference in the revised version is to the worst recorded storm tide.

(*b*) Where the original recommendations refer to the standard that would have been thought adequate prior to 1953, the revised version says the standard should be determined for each case so as to be commensurate with the benefits to be derived.

(c) An even higher standard (than the worst recorded) is not excluded where the property to be protected is of exceptional value, but anyone requiring such a standard may reasonably be expected to pay for it himself, unless it can be shown to be justified in terms of the general public interest.

(d) Similarly, where the value of the area to be protected is conspicuously below the general average, a lower standard is not excluded, but where people living under the protection of the defences in such an area have developed their property with those defences in view, they should, where practicable, be maintained.

(e) Allowance should be made (in design) for secular changes in sea level.

(f) Where the record is considered to be anomalous, the standard should be commensurate with that provided on adjacent parts of the coastline for similar circumstances.

At the same time as the Working Group to revise the Waverley Committee recommendations was set up, the Flood Protection Research Committee also set up a Working Group on Wave Heights under the chairmanship of Brian Trafford, and their Report is dealt with in Section 3.11.

The final version of the Revised Waverley Recommendations was prepared by G. Cole, then Chief Engineer, Ministry of Agriculture, Fisheries and Food, entitled *Sea Defence Standards* and combined in one short document the conclusions of the two Working Groups. This document is reproduced in Section 3.12.

3.11   REPORT OF WORKING GROUP ON WAVE HEIGHTS

The terms of reference of the Working Group on Wave Heights of the Flood Protection Research Committee were to consider the problem of determining design heights for sea defence works in respect of wave action.

Their Report commences with a recapitulation of current design practice and says that (for major schemes) the design of a defence should consider the effect of a wide spectrum of combinations of water levels and wave heights in terms of overtopping and possible breaching. Design should aim to make breaching an acceptably rare occurrence either by building to a height sufficient to minimise dangerous overtopping discharges or by armouring the landward face of the wall. The performance of a proposed design will then be assessed on the pattern of overtopping discharges to be expected. Generally the economic criterion will be that the present value of the expected flood damage avoided over the life of the structure will exceed the construction costs.

For urban design the concept is therefore of an 'unbreakable' defence that permits relatively minor flooding behind it from time to time. The wall is so armoured that breaching is most unlikely and the major design variable becomes the quantities of water allowed to go over the wall and the extents and frequencies of the corresponding floods so caused. The economic balance is between increasing expenditure on reducing overtopping and the reduced areas and frequencies of flooding so caused.

For rural design, the concept is one of a finite possibility of failure, resulting in a relatively large area of flooding. The walls are usually armoured to some degree, but the important design criterion is how much water can be accepted over the wall before failure. The economic balance is primarily between the costs of preventing failure and the damage to the area likely to be flooded when failure occurs.

For less exposed situations, for example within some estuaries where the fetch is limited, maximum wave height likely to be experienced can be determined by using recognised wind speed/fetch/wave height formulae. But for more major works, the design of the defence should consider the spectrum of combinations of water levels and wave heights. This is not seen as incompatible with Waverley Standards, but rather as stressing the need to confirm that the defences will be satisfactory under action of higher waves at lower levels.

Other factors referred to include the importance of taking into account the in-shore depths, since the deep sea waves will in many cases break either over underwater shoals or on the foreshore and re-form at lesser heights before finally breaking on the sea wall.

A procedure is suggested for design which is summarised as follows.

(a) Obtain return periods of tide levels (usually the Institute of Oceanographical Sciences would be able to advise on this).

(b) Knowing the wind directions to which the location is exposed, obtain estimates of the off-shore wind strengths, directions and durations for a range of probabilities (usually the Meteorological Office would be able to advise on this).

(c) From the wind data obtain corresponding wave height and period estimates at the off-shore location (usually the Institute of Oceanographical Sciences would be able to advise on this).

(d) From the off-shore wave data, estimate conditions inshore (usually the Hydraulics Research Station or other hydraulics laboratory would be able to advise on this).

(e) Combine the tide and wave data to obtain the return periods of combinations of tide levels and wave heights.

These design principles involve meteorological, oceanographic and hydraulics specialists, and since the final design will be based on a hydraulics model (either physical or numerical) it is suggested that it would seem logical for the hydraulics laboratory involved to act as liaison point for these specialists. From the model tests, the return periods of given overtopping discharges can be obtained.

The Report stresses the importance of taking into account, when obtaining the return periods of combinations of wave heights and tide levels, any correlation between the two events (see Section 1.16).

The Report concludes by making recommendations for further research.

The design procedures suggested by the Working Group are dealt with in greater detail in Sections 1.9, 1.15, 1.16 and 4.7.

3.12   REVISED SEA DEFENCE STANDARDS

These are set out in full, as issued by the Ministry of Agriculture, Fisheries and Food and are self-explanatory. The reader's attention is particularly drawn to the last paragraph. The design methods advocated in this book accord with the advice given in that paragraph.

105

3.12.1. Flood Protection Research Committee: sea defence standards

1 Since 1954 sea defence standards have generally followed the recommendations of the Waverley Committee. Following the floods of 1977 and 1978, it was suggested that these standards required revision. We have accordingly reviewed the situation and recommend as follows.

2 Where flooding would lead to serious damage to property of high value, such as valuable industrial premises or compact residential areas or where it would affect any large area of valuable agricultural land, the standard of defence should be such as to give protection from a recurrence of the worst recorded storm tide. In making this recommendation we had in mind the possibility of occurrence of an event of such extreme severity and rarity that to give protection against a recurrence would be grossly uneconomic. We would not wish to fetter the judgement of authorities or departments in deciding whether or not to spend public money on such protection and we therefore think that this recommendation should not be rigidly applied when return periods exceed about 1000 years.

3 In other areas where the value of the property to be protected is not sufficient to warrant so great an expense the standard should be determined for each case so as to be commensurate with the benefits to be derived.

4 An even higher standard is not excluded where the property to be protected is of exceptional value, but anyone requiring such a standard may reasonably be expected to pay for it himself, unless it can be shown to be justified in terms of the general public interest. Similarly, where the value of the area to be protected is conspicuously below the general average a lower standard is not excluded, but where people living under the protection of the defences in such an area have developed their property with those defences in view, they should, where practicable, be maintained.

5 Where the record is considered to be anomalous the standard should be commensurate with that provided on adjacent parts of the coastline for similar circumstances.

6 In observing these standards, due allowance should be made for secular changes in sea level.

7 It will be observed that paragraphs 2–4 follow closely the

106

format of the Waverley Committee's recommendations. We have substituted the phrase 'worst recorded storm tide' for the Waverley Committee's 1953 flood standard. We note that they defined this as the level of the tide plus surge. We recommend, however, that the revised standard should not be considered exclusively in terms of static water levels, but should take into account the effect of waves.

8 Before and since the acceptance of the recommendations of the Waverley Report it has generally been the practice to add an arbitrary 'freeboard'—frequently in the order of a metre—to the static water level to allow, among other things, for waves. Some authorities have also made use of techniques for estimating the size of waves likely to accompany the chosen combination of tide and surge. These techniques, however, disregard the possibility that the defences may be at greater risk from tides of lower static level combined with higher waves.

9 Researches since 1954 have shown that the criterion for flooding behind earth embankments is generally the overtopping level. The same standard obviously applies to 'hard' defences, such as concrete sea walls. Hence, and for the reasons given at paragraphs 7 and 8, we recommend that wave heights and static water levels at the design location and their estimated frequencies of occurrence be analysed together to assess frequencies of overtopping discharges. If waves occurring at lower static levels than those of the worst recorded storm tide are likely to impose more severe conditions, the worst combination should be used for design purposes.

3.13 INTERPRETATION OF REVISED STANDARDS

The method of obtaining the return periods of given wave heights occurring with given tide levels is explained in Section 1.16 (the second form of tabulation). If therefore the tide level and significant wave height are known (or the significant wave height accompanying the tide can be determined from the relevant meteorological data by the methods explained in Chapter 1), for an actual event, for example for the worst recorded storm tide referred to in the Revised Sea Defence Standards, then the return period of that event can be deduced.

Hence it is possible to interpret the Revised Sea Defence

Standards in terms of return period conditions, and this facilitates dealing with the situation, referred to in the Revised Sea Defence Standards, where records are considered to be anomalous (for example, records so short that the worst recorded storm tide is of very short return period). Hence the standard to be adopted is that commensurate with that provided on adjacent parts of the coastline for similar circumstances. This can therefore reasonably be interpreted that where the areas are similar, then the aim should be to design the scheme to withstand conditions of the same return period as that adopted for the corresponding area farther along the coast where records have been kept sufficiently long to provide a realistic value for the return period of the worst recorded storm tide.

3.14 PRACTICAL APPLICATION

On the philosophy basically set out in Section 3.13, the Southern Water Authority decided upon the following Standards of Defence against Tidal Flooding.

(*a*) Where flooding of extensive residential and valuable industrial areas would lead to serious damage and where there is a major risk to human life on a large scale, a 1 in 1000 year standard shall be adopted (Standard A).

(*b*) Where flooding would affect residential and industrial areas or large areas of valuable agricultural land, a 1 in 250 year standard shall be adopted (Standard B).

(*c*) Elsewhere, a 1 in 50 year standard shall be adopted (Standard C).

These standards are accompanied by the provisions that

(i) the date used for the return period shall be that corresponding to the end date of the design life of the structure

(ii) account must be taken of any secular changes in the sea level

(iii) if the recommended Standard cannot be justified economically then, except where over-riding considerations apply, the defences are to be built to the maximum Standard consistent with an acceptable cost/benefit ratio

(iv) the defences shall only be considered to be to the

required Standard if they will safely withstand those conditions and that overtopping (corresponding to that return period) is limited to an acceptable amount.

3.15   COUNTERWALLS AND CROSSWALLS

In many marsh areas counterwalls inland of the main sea defences exist which were built centuries ago as the main sea walls. Crosswalls also often exist between the first and second defence lines dividing the area liable to flooding into 'boxed' compartments.

The Waverley Committee recommended that these secondary defences, where serving a useful purpose, should be maintained and if necessary improved and that consideration should be given to the construction of new second-line defences where the potential benefit would justify the cost.

3.16   ACCESS

The Committee stressed the importance of providing easy access to sea defences at all times of flooding and pointed out that if access along the top of a wall or along a berm on the landward side were provided, the strength of the wall would be increased. Thus, usually the necessary strengthening of a wall can be combined with the provision of access. Crosswalls and counterwalls referred to in Section 3.15 may also be adapted to provide access at a high level across the marshes to the main sea walls.

3.17   OUTFALLS AND EVACUATION OF FLOOD WATER

The Committee drew attention to the need in many areas to provide outfalls to ensure the rapid evacuation of flood water. Such outfalls should often be much larger than necessitated by purely land-water drainage requirements. This recommendation applies particularly to built-up and industrial areas where evacuation of flood water in three days or so would enable rehabilitation and resumption of production to be effected quickly.

3.18 SEALING OFF TIDAL CREEKS

The Committee recommended that where there was no conflict with navigation or similar interests, consideration should be given to sealing off tidal creeks in order to obviate the need to maintain long lengths of creek walls.

3.19 WALL MATERIALS AND CONSTRUCTION
3.19.1 Clay

Clay is a common material for wall construction. In parts of Kent where there are difficulties in obtaining a good supply of clay, the seaward portions of the walls have been made of clay and the landward portions of more easily obtainable material such as a mixture of chalk and clinker. Other materials used are colliery waste and, with the advice of the Central Electricity Board, pulverized fuel ash.

In the past, the clay for walls has been taken mainly from adjoining delph ditches or borrow pits. Such material has usually a low shear strength, and its high moisture content often results in excessive shrinkage occurring. Hand placing permitted much moister clay to be used than is possible with bulldozers. Consequently present practice is to reduce the moisture content of marsh clay before placing it in the wall, or, alternatively, to use clay taken from hillside borrow pits which will be found usually to have more nearly the correct moisture content for compaction and can therefore often be placed straight into the wall. This imported clay is generally much stronger in shear strength and is often also found to contain a proportion of sand which keeps shrinkage to a minimum. Heavily pre-compressed (geologically) clays should be avoided, otherwise excessive expansion may cause bad fissuring.

The object of good earthwork embankment construction is to achieve maximum density by packing together the soil particles and expelling the air. Good compaction is ensured if the water content is slightly greater than the plastic limit. However, higher moisture content is sometimes specified (achieved if necessary by spraying with water as the work proceeds) in order to obtain the plasticity needed when substantial settlement is expected. If the moisture content is lower, voids remain in the wall, and if it is much higher, it is impossible to use normal mechanical compaction methods. As a rough guide it may be said that if the material is suitable for satisfactory movement and compaction by bulldozer, it has the correct moisture content for placing in the wall. A typical specification would be that the moisture content of the clay when compacted shall be 5–15% greater than the moisture content at its plastic limit.

3.19.2 Clay wall construction

Bulldozing is a very satisfactory method of placing and con-solidating clay in sea and river walls, but it is not practicable by this means to build a wall with side slopes much steeper than 2:1 (horizontal to vertical).

Imported clays can often be placed straight into the wall, but the moisture content of marsh clay must be reduced before it is placed. The material excavated should be spread for drying to a depth not exceeding 1 m and excavation and spreading should proceed in layers with the lowest and wettest material being placed on top. Top soil and turf need not be laid aside and may be incorporated in the heap.

The work can proceed throughout the year. During the summer period (May to October) when the material has dried sufficiently, it can be placed in its initial position in the wall, being taken from the heap by side-cut so that the layers are thoroughly mixed as they are moved. As filling in an improve-ment scheme proceeds, the existing wall should be lightly benched by side-cut with bulldozers in a series of steps as the fill is raised.

The initial placing should be at a gentle slope of, say, 4:1, forming a rough profile behind the existing wall. The following year it should be scarified to a depth of 0.5 to 1 m, recompacted and shaped to its final profile. Where the improvement is to the back of an existing wall, the landward edge of the crest should, in general, be left at least 150 mm higher than the designed level with a crossfall to seaward to allow for settlement. Finally, the top 150 mm of the surface can be brought to tilth, grass seed sown and rolled.

It was the common experience following the 1953 North Sea storm tide improvement works, that the grass sown was soon replaced by indigenous grasses, such as Couch Grass (*Agropyron repens*) and Sea Couch (*Agropyron pungens*).

This was confirmed by the results of field trials carried out for the Advisory Committee on Sea Defence Research between 1961 and 1964 in Essex and Suffolk. The Report (unpublished) concluded that unless there was a high standard of maintenance (not usually practicable on long lengths of sea defences) it was preferable to sow a non-persistent grass and encourage a controlled colonisation by indigenous grasses by lenient management practices.

A useful report published by CIRIA[13] recommends the following grass mixture for sea banks with low maintenance: 60% Creeping Red Fescue; 20% Hard Fescue; 20% Creeping Bent. Helpful advice can usually be obtained from the local office of the Agricultural Development and Advice Service, Ministry of Agriculture, Fisheries and Food, who will have valuable local knowledge.

When sub-soil conditions are poor and a firm stratum exists only at very great depth, considerable settlement must be expected and allowed for. Some of the tidal river walls in Kent are sinking at rates varying according to site from 25 mm to 75 mm a year. In such cases it is advisable to make the top of the wall 4.5–6.0 m wide. The wall can then be 'topped-up' every few years. When its top width has been reduced by this to about 3.0 m (minimum width for access along the top) major re-profiling works can be carried out at intervals of 10 to 30 years.

3.19.3 Sand wall construction

The customary method of placing sea-dredged sand is by hydraulic fill. Bunds are constructed, usually of material that can be incorporated in the finished structure, and then sand is pumped into the space formed by the bunds. Pumps are provided at the ends to evacuate the water. This method was used to form the landward berm of the improved Thames River Walls (Section 3.8). Lighters containing the sand were brought alongside a floating dredger, whence the sand was pumped ashore via a floating pipe-line.

Alternatively, a pontoon can be moored off-shore connected to the site by floating or submerged pipe-line. This enables suction dredgers equipped to pump out their cargoes to pump ashore by connecting to the seaward end of the pipeline on the pontoon.

Provided adequate arrangements are made for evacuating the water, it is possible for men and bulldozers to go onto the sand only minutes after it has been delivered. Final spreading and shaping is carried out by bulldozers.

REFERENCES

1 MARSLAND A. *Investigation by BRE of Problems associated with Flood Banks*. Report B 462/74. Garston, Building Research Establishment, 1974.

2 Various computer programs held by Genesys Ltd, Loughborough.

3 MARSLAND A. The design and construction of earthen flood banks. *J. Instn Wat. Engrs*, 1957, **11,** No. 3, May.

4 THORN R. B. *River Engineering and Water Conservation Works*. London, Butterworths, 1966.

5 HYDRAULICS RESEARCH STATION. *Model Study of a Precast Block Protective Apron for the Beach at Penrhyn Bay*. Report EX 462. Wallingford, Hydraulics Research Station, 1969.

6 OGINK H.J.M. *Investigations on Hydraulic Characteristics of Synthetic Fibres*. Report 146. Delft Hydraulics Laboratory, 1975.

7 BRITISH STANDARDS INSTITUTION. *Aggregates from Natural Sources for Concrete*, BS 882: part 2: 1973 metric units. London, British Standards Institution, 1973.

8 PARRY R.H.G. Field and laboratory behaviour of a lightly over-consolidated clay. *Géotechnique*, 1968, **18,** No. 2, 151–171.

9 BURLAND, J.B. *Pore pressures and Displacements beneath Embankments on Soft Natural Clay Deposits*. Current paper 6/72. Garston, Building Research Establishment, 1972.

10 VOLD R.C. *Undisturbed Sampling of Soils*. Publication 17. Oslo, Norwegian Geotechnical Institute, 1956.

11 TERZAGHI K. and PECK R.B. *Soil Mechanics in Engineering Practice*, 2nd edn, 116–117. New York, J. Wiley, 1948.

12 HMSO. *Report of the Departmental Committee on Coastal Flooding*. London, HMSO, 1954.
13 WHITEHEAD E. *A Guide to the Use of Grass in Hydraulic Engineering Practice*. Technical note 71. London, Construction Industry Research and Information Association.

Chapter 4

The hydraulic design of wall profiles and revetment details

4.1 GENERAL CONSIDERATIONS

Estuarial flood embankments are usually protected against severe wave action by the estuary itself and by the saltings which are often at a higher level than the land protected by the wall. Rice grass is widely used to resist erosion and assist accretion of the saltings (see Section 2.13).

The top of a clay wall should preferably be at least 1 m above highest known tide level so that the risk of water flowing through the surface fissures is minimized. It should be correspondingly higher if considerable wave action is expected.

Soil mechanics, standards of protection and similar considerations are dealt with in Chapter 3, and this Chapter is concerned mainly with profile and revetment design from hydraulic and structural considerations. If the soil is such that the desirable level for the top of the wall cannot be attained without rotational slip occurring, then alternatives are possible. One is to construct a crest wall (details of such designs are given in this book) combined if necessary with weighting berms on the seaward and/or landward sides. Another alternative, sometimes combined with the first, is to provide adequate protection to the back of the wall, so that it may be overtopped without damage at high tide during severe storms. In many cases the period of overtopping is short, occurring only at the peak of the tide and the quantity of water passing over the wall is often comparatively small, so that it can be absorbed in marshlands by the extensive dyke system and discharged to the sea through gravity outfalls as the tide falls. For industrial and residential areas, overtopping must be kept to acceptably low volumes at infrequent intervals consistent with cost/benefit justification.

A common batter for the front of earthen estuarial walls is 3 : 1 (horizontal to vertical) and 2½ : 1 for the rear. The practical limit is about 2 : 1 if modern means of construction by bulldozer are used. Flatter slopes have often to be employed on the seaward face, particularly on exposed lengths and on the landward face also if overtopping is expected where no special protection other than good turf is provided. These aspects are dealt with in greater detail later in this Chapter and also in Chapter 3.

Protection against attrition by wave action caused by wind or wash from navigation may take the form of brushwood faggots (which also assist accretion of silt), of dumped or pitched stone, of sheet piling or of concrete blocks. Usually an essential requirement of all forms of revetment for river, estuary and sea walls is flexibility, since slow settlement of one or other of the types described in Chapter 3 occurs on many of these walls. Where settlement is not expected, protection can be given by fabric mattresses which are laid on the riverward face and then filled by pumping with cement/sand grout. These can be provided with mesh filters or with weep-holes where required.

On the larger sea walls, the blockwork is usually contained in panels, so that if a washout occurs, the spread of the damage is limited. On the foreshore, the panel walls often consist of timber or steel sheet piling and a toe wall of sheet piling is frequently used. On the main part of the seaward face where settlement may be expected and where tide levels do not present great constructional difficulties, the panels are usually of reinforced concrete with hinge joints to ensure flexibility.

4.2   TYPES OF SEA WALL

Sea walls may be divided into two main classes, those from which waves are reflected and those on which waves break. It is generally agreed that any intermediate type that gives a combination of reflection and breaking sets up very severe erosive action of the sea bed in front of the wall. A slope of about 2 : 1 is the steepest on which waves will properly break (see Section 1.11), dissipating the wave energy in turbulence in breaking and in run up.

The second category can be sub-divided into two main sub-groups, (*a*) those where the depth of water in front of the wall is such that waves break on the structure and (*b*) those where the bigger waves break on the foreshore in front of the wall.

The Northern sea wall and the Dymchurch sea wall are examples of type (*a*) (Figs. 67 and 38) and the Seasalter sea wall (Fig. 61) is an example of type (*b*).

4.3   APRON SLOPES AND BERMS

The general effect of flattening the slope is to lessen the swash height, lessen foreshore erosion and reduce the wave pressure on the upper part of the apron. It therefore follows that the smaller the depth of water in front of the wall at high tide (and hence the smaller the waves that can approach it) and the more inerodible the foreshore, the steeper the revetment can be. The slope may therefore vary from 2 : 1 (horizontal to vertical) for an estuary wall well protected by a wide salting at a high level and by the estuary (the 2 : 1 slope being about the practical limit from earthwork constructional considerations) to 5 : 1 or even flatter for a sea wall in deep water that permits large waves to approach and break on the wall. It will also have been seen from Sections 1.11 and 1.17 that if the apron is steeper than 2 : 1 then generally the wave will not break but will be reflected, usually causing intense disturbance of the foreshore.

In the past, elliptical (or parabolic) profiles have been popular. Frequently, in the cases of the higher walls this has been considered to entail an excessive parabolic development and the lower part of the apron has been of uniform slope. The considerations to be taken into account in deciding seaward revetment profiles are now described. The golden rule should be, if there is doubt or disagreement as to the best profile to adopt, not to be dogmatic but to carry out model tests on the alternatives and from the results to determine the most suitable design.

The sea walls at Dymchurch in Kent provide interesting information on apron slopes, since with their varying profiles they can be regarded as full-scale models tested over the years by the worst combinations of conditions. On the length from

Fig. 37. Northern sea wall model under test

Grand Redoubt to Willop, the apron was made steeper many years ago, to a slope of 4½ : 1. At highest recorded tide level there was about 6 m of water in front of the wall. The wall has suffered considerable damage by wave action and the sand foreshore in front of it has dropped to the lowest level for this part of the coast. However, the wall adjoining it immediately south of Willop which is elliptical in profile and of similar construction but of flatter slope (average slope of main part of apron 7½ : 1), has no history of damage. It also maintains a much higher foreshore in front of it (the foreshore level changes rapidly over a short length at the change in apron section). This latter point stresses the need for flat slopes to limit disturbance of the natural foreshores, particularly those of sand, to a minimum.

Undoubtedly, the steeper the slope the greater the wave reflection, and hence the greater the turbulence in front of the wall. This creates a lower sand level by putting more sand in suspension, which is carried by the tidal currents and deposited on adjoining lengths where the slope of the apron is flatter and the turbulence less. The effect of impermeable structures on foreshore stability is discussed in Section 2.3.

It is common practice to put a berm on the seaward side of the wall at about the level of high water. For maximum effectiveness it is found that the berm width should be about one fifth of the wave length. Tests on the Northern sea wall model (see Fig. 37), showed that when an 11 m wide berm was added no great improvement was observed for waves of 10 s period, but conditions were materially improved for waves of 6 and 8 s period. Wave heights taken in the tests range from 1 to 4.2 m.

118

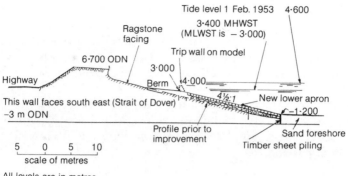

Fig. 38. Dymchurch sea wall profile, Grand Redoubt to Willop

Little information is available about the effects of berms at levels below high water, although it will be obvious that such berms would be much cheaper to construct. On the front of one length of wall at All Hallows in North Kent, a berm was built of width approximately one quarter the wave length and at a level below high water approximately equal to the wave height. Experience has shown this to be very effective in reducing wave action on the pitching, this length remaining undamaged at times when quite extensive damage has occurred to the pitching on the lengths on either side of it. Thorndike Saville's method (Section 1.18) may often be used with advantage in initial studies of the possible behaviour of profiles of this type.

Fig. 38 shows the improvement carried out on the Dymchurch sea wall on the length from Grand Redoubt to Willop. Model tests at the Hydraulics Research Station, Wallingford showed that the berm was most effective in reducing wave action on the upper part of the apron and in assisting the reduction of water passing over the wall. Tests on alternative profiles showed this one to be most satisfactory and its adoption served a fourfold purpose: (*a*) strengthening of the lower apron that had been weakened by severe abrasion; (*b*) reduction in wave action on the upper part of the apron, thereby removing the need to carry out expensive strengthening works on that part; (*c*) reduction of overtopping, thus reducing the risk of damage

119

to the unprotected landward face of the wall; and (*d*) provision of an access berm for plant for groyne and wall maintenance, of great value since the distance from wave wall to toe is too great for the reach of normal cranes. The waves reproduced in the tests were of 6, 7, 8 and 9 s periods and of heights varying from 0.7 to 3.9 m.

Above the berm or above high water it is frequently the practice to steepen the slope, and slopes of 3 : 1 for (*a*) type walls (see Section 4.2) and 2 : 1 for (*b*) type walls are common for this upper portion.

4.4 STEPWORK, WAVE WALLS, TRIP WALLS AND ROUGHNESS BLOCKS

Fig. 37 shows the model of the Northern sea wall under test at the Neyrpic Laboratories, Grenoble, and under the severe conditions reproduced in the test, with the wave wall height much less than the wave height, the ineffectiveness of the stepwork and curved wave wall will be seen.

Curved wave walls are however more effective under less severe conditions and much superior to vertical wave walls. As a very general rule, the wave wall height should preferably be not less than the wave height. Fig. 40 shows a curved wave wall operating very effectively in the three-dimensional model tests (which permitted obliquity of the waves to be studied) with random waves for the exposed part of the Medway Estuary wall at Sheerness. A vertical wave wall of the same height threw water vertically high into the air (which an on-shore wind would carry landwards).

Where circumstances make it practicable to do so, it is preferable to place the curved wave wall on the landward side of the crest rather than on the seaward side. A good example of this was the case of the pilot model tests for the (northern) wall at Sheerness. The then existing wall had a 2 : 1 seaward apron, a 9 m wide promenade about 150 mm above the 1954 tide level and an 0.5 m high landward wall. With this tide level and waves 1.5 m high, period 6 s, the model showed large quantities of water overtopping the wall. But with a 1.3 m high curved wave wall on the landward side of the promenade, very little overtopping occurred. The 1.3 m wave wall was then placed on the seaward side of the promenade and under the

120

same conditions large quantities of water were thrown upwards at the wave wall, which, under prototype conditions would be carried landwards by the onshore wind.

Reverting to stepwork, it was decided not to use it for the Northern sea wall (which is between Reculver and Birchington) because of the results of the model test, and because shingle at the site would in any case have abraded the arrises. Recent tests show, even with large waves, stepwork can under some conditions reduce overtopping and tests to check this can be made. For less exposed sea walls on sandy foreshores, where abrasion is not severe, stepwork is more durable and has the merit of reducing swash height and scour at the toe under less severe conditions.

At the Hydraulics Research Station, Wallingford, a trip wall (shown in broken line on Fig. 38) was added to the Dymchurch sea wall model to ascertain its effects. It was found that at extra high tide all waves both large and small broke with considerable impact on the trip wall, sending spray in all directions, a great deal of which on the prototype would be carried over the wall by the onshore wind to damage the landward face of the wall.

Roughness blocks in the form of cylinders 1.2 m in diameter with 1.2 m spaces between them were also tried, but again these greatly increased the amount of spray thrown into the air and were therefore considered undesirable, quite apart from their obvious shortcomings from amenity and aesthetic aspects.

As distinct from large roughness blocks, aprons with rough surfaces such as roughly laid stone have the advantage that they can reduce the swash height by up to about 15%. As explained above, stepwork can also reduce swash height, but it can also cause large quantities of spray to be thrown into the air to be carried landwards by the on-shore wind and this can be undesirable if a road or dwellings exist in the vicinity of the landward toe of the wall.

4.5   EFFECT OF WAVE ACTION ON BLOCKWORK

The seaward face of the Dymchurch sea wall model (Fig. 38) was made of rigid materials except for one line of loosely held

blocks 11 mm square and 13 mm deep, approximately equivalent to 300 mm cubes in the prototype. They sat in cubical
holes 13 mm square and 13 mm deep and the movement of the
blocks was regarded as a measure of the wave attack. Waves
greater than 0.7 m (prototype dimension) in height removed
cubes at the point where the waves plunged, while waves 0.7 m
high removed one cube. The number of cubes removed was
taken as a measure of the wave attack.

The ease with which waves of small height removed 300 mm
cubes showed that the strength of the apron did not lie so much
in the weight of the individual stones as in the water-tightness
and strength of the mortar jointing the stones.

4.6 EFFECT OF WAVE ACTION ON INTERLOCKING BLOCKS

Further tests in connection with the Dymchurch Sea Wall
were carried out on a panel representing 380 mm × 380 mm ×
200 mm interlocking blocks of the Kent type (described in Sections 4.13 and 4.14). The linear scale was 1:24 and the density
scale 1:1. Waves representing prototype waves of 7 s period
were reproduced. Waves of small height were first generated
with the level of still-water low, and the water level was then
slowly raised until the waves were breaking well above the
panel of blocks. If no blocks were removed, the wave height
was increased and the experiment repeated until a block was
pulled out. It was observed that quite small waves disturbed
individual blocks or small areas of the panel without removing
them and after each disturbance they fell back again into position.

It was found that the resistance of the blocks to movement
was dependent on the tightness with which they fitted into the
panel.

When there was no clearance between the blocks, no wave
that could be reproduced (up to a maximum of 2.8 m in height)
pulled blocks out. When the total clearance between all the
blocks in a row (of eight or nine blocks per row) was 0.25 mm,
or 6 mm in prototype dimensions, the smallest wave that
pulled blocks out was found to be either 1.8 m high or 1.4 m
high depending on the conditions round the edge of the panel.
Greater clearance between the blocks resulted in poorer resist-

ance to wave attack. The alternative conditions round the edge of the panel represented, first, concrete effectively bonding the peripheral blocks to the frame, and second, concrete not bonding these blocks to the frame and allowing movement, that is the outside edges of the blocks forming the perimeter of the panel were filed so that they were free to slide up and down in the frame.

This set of experiments demonstrated the importance of the interlocking, or in the case of plain blocks, of the strength of the mortar jointing the blocks, in determining the ability of a revetment to withstand wave action.

4.7 PROBABILISTIC DESIGN FOR GIVEN RETURN PERIOD CONDITIONS (RELATED TO OVERTOPPING)

From the results of calculating the return periods of various combinations of tide level and wave height (second form of tabulation in Section 1.16), a curve can be drawn for any given return period of r years, with the x axis representing wave height and the y axis representing tide level. This is useful for considering the wave action that could occur on a structure designed to withstand r years return period conditions, and for model tests on coast protection structures when, because of cliffs immediately behind, there is no overtopping. It is important to appreciate that although over a very long period of time each of these combinations of wave height and tide level has individually a return period of r years, more than one of these combinations could occur in a period of r years with its associated overtopping. Such curves cannot therefore be used for determining for any given wall profile the return period of a stated rate of overtopping being equalled or exceeded.

Design therefore proceeds as follows. Having decided, provisionally, the desirable standard for the scheme, for example that overtopping rate should not equal or exceed a permissible figure more often than once on average every r_1 years, and from the preliminary studies having ascertained that it is likely to be economically viable (see Sections 4.27–4.32), the next step is to model test the trial wall profile.

As an example, the procedure used by the Hydraulics Research Station for Llandulas where the profiles tested consisted

123

of (a) a simple 2:1 sloping apron of dolosse and (b) the same, but with a berm, was as follows. If the mean overtopping discharge $\bar{Q}$ per metre length is measured in the model for various values of $\bar{H}_s$, $\bar{P}_r$, still water levels and wall crest levels, R being the difference in levels between the crest and the still water level, then it can be shown[1-3] that if $\bar{Q}/g\bar{H}_s\,\bar{P}_r$ (the dimensionless discharge) is plotted against $R/\bar{P}_r\,(g\bar{H}_s)^{1/2}$ (the dimensionless freeboard), the results should form a band for which the upper boundary envelope curve can be drawn.

Wave breaking over a sea-bed profile is characterised in irregular waves by S, Battjes' steepness parameter (typical value could be 0.05), where $S = 2\pi\bar{H}_s/g\bar{P}_r^2$. The higher the value of S, the more the waves break, until an upper limit is reached where higher waves cannot occur because of breaking. It was found, for Llanddulas, that for the 39 events on average per annum, S could reasonably be taken at a constant value. With this constant value of S, for any value of $\bar{H}_s$, $\bar{P}_r$ can be found from the above expression. Hence for an assumed value of profile crest level and for any tide level and wave height combination tabulated, $R/\bar{P}_r(g\bar{H}_s)^{1/2}$ can be calculated, and hence from the envelope curve, the value of $\bar{Q}/g\bar{H}_s\bar{P}_r$ can be read, from which, with $\bar{H}_s$ and $\bar{P}_r$ known, $\bar{Q}$ can be calculated.

Basically, the same procedure was used by the Hydraulics Research Station for their Fleetwood sea wall study.[3] It was also used for the Sheerness northern wall (Fig. 64) except that the curve for a given crest level was derived by the method of least squares. For the Sheerness western wall (Fig. 40) two curves were found necessary, one for the tide at the levels of the vertical wall and one where it was below these (Hydraulics Research Station Reports Ex 947, 1980 and Ex 923, 1980, Design of sea walls and model tests to determine overtopping).

Referring now to the first tabulation set out in Section 1.16 (page 22), the next step is to underline *all* the probabilities in the table that correspond to wave height/tide level combinations at which the permissible overtopping is equalled or exceeded. The sum of these underlined probabilities is the probability of the permissible overtopping being reached or exceeded. Alternatively, consecutive overtopping rate ranges can be selected, and for each of these the probabilities of wave/tide combinations with rates in the range can be underlined and summated to give the probabilities of those overtopping rate ranges. The corresponding return period is obtained from the expression $r = i/p$ (see Section 1.16). If the return period so arrived at corresponds to the design return period, then the trial wall profile could be accepted initially as appropriate. Subsequently checks can be made that structurally the wall will withstand the combinations of tide levels and wave heights whose probabilities contribute to the sum of the probabilities. If not, then the assumed level of the trial wall can be raised or lowered and the procedure repeated.

If the trial profile assumed seems to be appropriate, the next step is to take suitable percentages of the permissible overtopping and then repeat the procedure to determine the return periods of these lesser rates. A graph can then be plotted of overtopping discharge rate equalled or exceeded against return period.

The calculations so far have been concerned with rates of overtopping, and combinations of tide level and wave height have been underlined in the matrix which corresponded to the permissible overtopping being equalled or exceeded.

If any chosen tide level is taken as the top of the tide, then from the foregoing, for any associated wave height, the rate of overtopping is known. If then the tide level underneath it in the tabulation is taken, the rate of overtopping with that level and the same wave height is also known. Next, if from the tide curve the time intervals as the tide rises to high water and drops back again to the lower level are ascertained, then the volume of overtopping in the time intervals can be estimated. The calculation can then be repeated for the next lower tide level and so on. If it is found that for the cells of the matrix the ratio of volume of overtopping to rate of overtopping is reasonably constant, then use of this ratio for converting rate to volume will save a considerable amount of time.

Hence, as an alternative, for each combination of high tide level and wave height, not only is the rate of overtopping on the top of the tide known, but also the volume of overtopping as the tide rises and falls. Substituting volumes therefore for rates, the procedure can be repeated, by underlining those probabilities which correspond to the permissible volume being equalled or exceeded, and therefore the return period of that volume being

125

equalled or being exceeded can be calculated.

Thus a stage will have been reached where it will be possible to indicate the extents, depths, and frequencies of the reduced flooding likely to result from the proposed improvement scheme. This information would also be used in the detailed cost/benefit justification for the scheme (see Sections 4.27 to 4.32).

Alternatively, the third form of tabulation given in Section 1.16 on page 24 may be used to determine the return period of given overtopping being reached or exceeded. From the model results, determine for each tide level the wave height at which the given overtopping is *first* reached or exceeded. On the Table, underline the corresponding combined probabilities; the sum of the underlined probabilities is then the probability of the given overtopping being reached or exceeded. It should be noted that, unlike the first form of tabulation, with this third form of tabulation, only one figure will be underlined in each vertical column, because the figures in the tabulation are cumulative.

As an alternative to specifying return periods of overtopping being reached or exceeded, it is possible to specify that the overtopping must be reduced to at least a given fraction, say one tenth. Overtopping is plotted against return period for curves representing the existing wall and various heights of improved wall profiles. A further curve is then plotted representing the chosen fraction of the overtopping of the existing wall. Finally, from the curves, the improved profile height can be selected (or interpolated) that gives this reduction.

This relative reduction method was employed by the Hydraulics Research Station in their Fleetwood sea wall investigations.[3] Curves can of course be plotted for both statistically dependent and statistically independent assumptions. Referring to the Fleetwood investigations, the Hydraulics Research Station Annual Report[2] for 1979 comments 'This method (that is, the relative reduction method) has the advantage that the choice of statistical interdependency of the wave heights and water levels and the value of S become relatively insignificant.'

This Section covers particular applications of probabilistic design to sea defence and coast protection works. For a more general statement of probabilistic design in its widest sense, applied to maritime works, the reader is referred to work by Dover and Bea.[4]

4.8 REGULAR AND IRREGULAR WAVES IN MODELS

The general characteristics of regular waves and irregular waves (random waves) are set out in Section 1.11. Model testing at one time was carried out using trains of regular waves (uniform waves) of the same wave height as the significant wave height to be expected in the prototype. This approach has its limitations. For example, it is now known that overtopping may be very much more if irregular waves of significant wave height equal to the wave height of regular waves are used in a model. For this reason, irregular waves are used these days in such models.

It has been seen in Section 1.11 that wave heights and periods vary randomly according to probability distributions characterised by the wave spectrum (energy spectrum) from which the probability distributions can be obtained. So one approach, if recorded wave data are not available, is to use a standard spectrum such as the Pearson–Moskowitz spectrum[5] with the design parameters $\bar{H}_s$ and $\bar{P}_r$ (or $\bar{P}_s$) to specify the energy spectrum required for the model investigation, since it is possible to relate the spectrum to these parameters.

The Pearson–Moskowitz spectrum is a fully developed spectrum based on North Atlantic data. Where a fetch-limited spectrum would be more suitable, the Joint North Sea Wave Project (JONSWAP) spectrum is available. If recorded wave data are available, the spectrum can be obtained from these.

The wave spectrum in itself does not provide information about the actual succession of the waves, that is, the wave patterns. Investigations by the Hydraulics Research Station (Annual Report, 1977), show that structures respond differently when exposed to different wave patterns and this is important, for example, in connection with overtopping studies and stability of armour units. In such cases it is important to ensure that the wave patterns appear with the same relative frequency in the model as in the prototype. The occurrence and frequency of characteristic patterns in wave records must therefore be

127

studied and the results incorporated if necessary into the sea conditions used in the model investigations.

These circumstances could perhaps be the exception rather than the rule. It has been found that the frequencies of wave groups for a number of wave spectra (Moskowitz, JONSWAP and a bimodal spectrum generated using the HRS synthesiser) compare very favourably with published field data.[6]

Some random wave generators reproduce wave by wave from wave records, while others reproduce the random sea from the wave spectrum and build in phase shift to produce the required grouping. For a discussion on hinged generators, see reference 7.

A good example of model proving, simulating random waves, is at the port of Acajutla, El Salvador.[8] The swell spectrum measured off-shore by wave-rider buoy was used as input to the random wave generator. This generated the actual sea state both in regard to its spectral content, that is, the way in which wave height is distributed over various frequencies and in its irregular appearance, or the way consecutive waves vary in height.

Waves were then measured at the tip of the pier in the model and compared with those measured at the site. Reasonable agreement was obtained, but long waves in the model were found to be much smaller than the corresponding waves measured at the site.

Consequently, the amount of long-period motion was adjusted until it generated a long wave component in the model that agreed with that measured at the site.

This procedure had to be adopted because wave-rider buoys do not respond to long waves with periods of the order of one minute or more and thus the long wave activity outside the port was not picked up.

With this adjustment, agreement between model and prototype was found to be good.

4.9   BASIC PRINCIPLES OF MODELS

Mobile bed models are highly specialised. Examples of such models, used for investigating the behaviour of groynes and permeable groynes are given in Section 2.6, and of the effects of sea walls on shingle and on sand foreshores in Section 2.3. The use of numerical models for determining refraction is described in Section 1.13.

Rigid bed models are those most commonly used in relation to sea defence and coast protection works. Examples are: (*a*) to determine the effects of wave action on stepwork, aprons, berms, wave walls, trip walls and roughness blocks (see Sections 4.3 and 4.4); (*b*) to determine the degree of wave attack on profiles and the effects of wave action on blockwork (see Section 4.5) and on interlocking blockwork (see Section 4.6); and (*c*) to investigate either qualitatively or quantitatively the overtopping of sea walls. The Northern Sea Wall model (see Section 4.4) was an example of the former and the Sheerness Sea Wall model was an example of the latter. When quantitative results are required, the maximum rate of overtopping on the top of the tide and also the total volume of overtopping as the tide rises to and falls from the high water level, are usually determined.

Since, in deep water, wave velocity is a function of the wave length and in shallow water, a function of the depth of the water, models are made to natural scales, that is, geometrically similar to the prototype. There is a limit to the smallness of the models, for if the scale is of the order of 1/150 or less the wave characteristics will probably be affected by friction and surface tension.

In making models and interpreting the results, it is essential to grasp clearly the inherent limitations of this approach to design and the following is a short summary of the basic ideas on which model experimentation is founded.

The principle of dynamical similarity requires that all forces acting on the prototype and model should be in the same ratio. From Newton's second law, force = mass × acceleration. If suffixes p and m denote prototype and model, respectively, and F_p/F_m be written F_r, then

$$F_r = M_r a_r = \rho_r L_r^3 \frac{L_r}{T_r^2} = \rho_r L_r^2 V_r^2 \qquad (4.1)$$

With hydraulic models, three basic forces have usually to be considered, namely gravity, viscosity and surface tension.

If, as for sea walls, the only force acting is gravity, because

129

Fig. 39.   Testing in Wave Basin with irregular waves (Crown copyright; reproduced by permission Controller HMSO, courtesy Hydraulics Research Station, Wallingford)

by ensuring the scale is considerably greater than 1/150, the other forces are kept negligible in comparison, then $F_r = \rho_r L_r^3 g_r$. Equating this to equation (4.1)

$$\frac{V_r^2}{L_r g_r} = 1 \quad \text{or} \quad \frac{V_p^2}{L_p g_p} = \frac{V_m^2}{L_m g_m}$$

where $V/(Lg)^{1/2}$ is the dimensionless Froude Number, from which it follows that the Froude Number must be the same for model and prototype. V_p/V_m is therefore equal to $[(L_p g_p)/(L_m g_m)]^{1/2}$.

Sea wall models using water and geometrically similar to the prototype will therefore have the same Froude Number for model and prototype, since V_m/V_p will equal $L_m^{1/2}/L_p^{1/2}$ which equals $(L_m g)^{1/2}/(L_p g)^{1/2}$ or, $V_m/(L_m g)^{1/2} = V_p/(L_p g)^{1/2}$, that is, the Froude Number for the model is equal to that of the prototype.

Hence, if the linear scale L_m/L_p is $1/S$, the velocity scale V_m/V_p is $1/S^{1/2}$, the discharge scale (for overtopping tests) Q_m/Q_p is equal to $1/S^{3/2}$ and the time scale is $1/S^{1/2}$.

Preliminary wall profiles should be designed in accordance with the general principles set out in this Chapter. Alternative

130

Fig. 40.   Western wall, Sheerness, under test, showing effect of curved wave wall (Crown copyright; reproduced by permission Controller HMSO, courtesy Hydraulics Research Station, Wallingford)

designs can then be tested by models to determine the most suitable.

The subject of regular and random waves in models is discussed in Section 4.8 and an example is given of random wave model proving.

The northern wall at Sheerness and the western wall (Medway Estuary wall) at Sheerness investigations are examples of the use of irregular waves in quantitative (overtopping) models. The wall profiles were tested in a wave basin rather than a wave flume because it was necessary to study the effects of obliquity of approach of the waves.

Fig. 39 shows the wave basin and Fig. 40 the western wall, under test.

Other similar examples of overtopping model investigations are those for the Llanddulas and Fleetwood sea walls described in Section 4.7 (which explains how the return periods of given overtopping are obtained from the results of the model tests).

Fig. 41.   Keyed ragstone pitching

Physical models (with exaggerated vertical scales) and numerical models are also used for predicting the reflected waves from closure of tidal barriers and the increase in tide levels resulting from raising tidal embankments with consequent reduction in overtopping.

4.10   STONE PITCHING

Stone pitching is an ancient form of protection to estuary walls and consists of stone (in Kent usually ragstone of nominal thickness 225 mm) properly placed on the clay face of the wall and keyed by wedge-shaped stones firmly driven into place. Revetments of this type are flexible and have proved very satisfactory in the past. They are, in fact, often found superior to flexible concrete blockwork under conditions where excessive local movement of the apron may be expected. Fig. 41 shows a length of keyed ragstone pitching on a length of wall at Upchurch on the Medway Estuary. The difficulty these days is to find sufficient skilled men capable of carrying out the work.

Alternatives to the skilled process of keying when laying new

Fig. 42.   Asphalt jointed pitching

work are to grout the blocks with asphalt or to brush in a weak cement/sand grout (say 1:8). In the latter case, cracks appear if there is settlement, which can easily be cut out and regrouted as a part of routine maintenance. Asphalt jointing is particularly suitable when greater settlement and degree of exposure are expected, and provides a flexible apron. If it is used the stones should be clean and should be primed before grouting with a 50/50 blend of bitumen and white spirit, otherwise the asphalt may tend to come away from the stone. The specification of asphalt for sea defence work is a matter for specialists and expert advice can always be obtained from petroleum companies that supply bitumen. Terms used in asphalt work are defined in Section 4.17.

The most suitable composition naturally depends on the climatic temperature, aspect (whether facing north or south, for example), the slope of the pitching and the size of the joints. As an indication of the proportions likely to be used for this type of work, a suitable compound for use in England on pitching laid at a normal slope would be by weight 47% bitumen of 20/30 penetration, 47% sand (passing a 10 mesh sieve but retained on a 200 mesh sieve) and 6% asbestos fibres. Fig. 42 shows asphalt jointed pitching on the Isle of Sheppey.

For roughly laid stone or slag an asphalt comprising 73%

133

sand, 10% filler (minimum 70% passing 200 mesh sieve) and 17% bitumen of 60/70 penetration would be suitable in many cases.

Suitable stable cold emulsions are sometimes used as an alternative to hot bituminous compounds. They have the advantage that often the sand need not be dried (unless it is very wet) and heating is obviated. An appropriate grout would be 1 litre of suitable proprietary cold emulsion to $0.01\,m^3$ of sand.

It is common also to add Portland cement to the mix; this causes dehydration throughout the mass and the initial set occurs quickly, in under an hour. A suitable mix for jointing packed stone would be by weight of the order 70% sand, 8% cement and 22% bitumen emulsion. Again expert advice is necessary in any particular case and for any specific proprietary cold binder.

4.11 GRANITE BLOCKWORK AND CONCRETE BLOCKWORK

Granite blockwork is one of the finest forms of revetment for resisting severe abrasion. Relative durabilities and relative costs of various types of blockwork are given in Section 4.19, from which the value of granite will be evident. It is obviously essential to provide a good mortar. For 300 mm thick blocks the following would be satisfactory: 1 volume sulphate-resisting cement to 2½ volumes all-in granite aggregate (to Table 3 of BS 1201) to 2% by weight (of cement) calcium chloride, together with sufficient air-entraining agent to provide 3–5% by volume of entrained air (for workability with low water/cement ratio). Alternatives to granite are other igneous rocks such as basalt.

Fig. 43 gives details of 15 in × 15 in × 14 in (380 mm × 380 mm × 355 mm) concrete blocks for use where settlement is not expected. The shape of the joints 'locks' in the jointing mortar. Blocks of this type were used for the reconstruction of the Dymchurch sea wall (Fig. 38). They were made of gap-graded concrete which tests showed was at least equal to continuously graded concrete with regard to frost and sulphate resistance, and materially superior with regard to abrasion resistance.

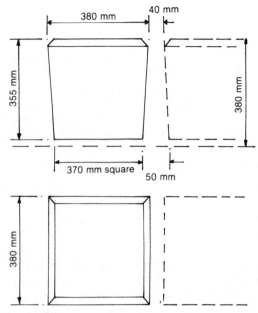

Fig. 43.   Details of Dymchurch sea wall type blocks

The aggregates for the mix were 40 mm single size coarse aggregate and 5 mm down sand, all to BS 882. The mix was, by weight, 78% coarse aggregate, 22% sand, aggregate/cement ratio 5.5. With a water/cement ratio of 0.37 and using rapid-hardening cement, this gave a mean compressive strength at 7 days of 55.1 N/mm^2, which corresponds to over 62 N/mm^2 at 28 days. The required minimum strength at 28 days, using rapid hardening cement, was 47 N/mm^2—the corresponding value for ordinary Portland cement being 41.5 N/mm^2. Assuming, with very high control, a value of 83% for the minimum strength as percentage of average strength, an average strength at 28 days of at least 56.5 N/mm^2 was needed. Therefore this mix was considered satisfactory. Subsequent site tests showed this assumption to be justified.

The mortar for these blocks was as recommended for granite blockwork but substituting crushed stone or gravel (in quality conforming to the requirements of BS 882 but in grading to Table 3 of BS 1201) in place of the granite aggregate.

135

4.12   FREE BLOCKS AND DESIGN OF MONOLITHIC APRONS

The first step is to determine the maximum height of wave that will break on the apron under the standard of return period conditions adopted. For these conditions, the studies carried out in accordance with Sections 1.16 and 4.7 will have provided the wave heights to be expected with various tide levels, corrected for refraction and, where necessary, for the effects of off-shore underwater sand banks (see Sections 1.11 and 1.14).

For each combination of tide level and wave height, the depth of water over the foreshore seaward of the toe of the wall must be ascertained to ensure that the wave concerned would not in fact break further out on the foreshore instead of on the wall. Relevant expressions for this exercise are given in Section 1.11. It will often be found that the depth of water over the foreshore is the factor which determines the height of the largest wave that will break on the wall. Investigations on these lines will give the wave height to be adopted for design of the apron.

Wave pressures on sloping aprons are referred to in Section 1.20, but it is not possible to design the apron thickness directly from this information.

In this Section, 'monolithic aprons' means in situ concrete aprons, or aprons composed of concrete blocks or stone blocks set in bituminous or cement/sand mortar (for asphalt concrete aprons, see Section 3.5). It would appear that *very* roughly, a wave will move in an apron a loose block of concrete of thickness about one third the off-shore wave height, or, correspondingly, on a steep slope, approximately one sixth of the breaking wave height, since on a steep slope the breaking wave height can be up to twice the deep water height. Hence a liberal approach would seem to be for *monolithic* aprons to use these ratios for determining the apron thickness, plus due allowance where necessary for abrasion losses during the life of the structure. (It will be seen from Section 4.15 that the Hydraulics Research Station suggest this one sixth of the breaking wave height approach in the design of their interlocking blocks on steep slopes.)

As in the case of rubble breakwaters, it would seem acceptable in design of monolithic aprons to take the off-shore significant wave height, it being considered that if the apron is stable for waves of the significant wave height, then the occasional single large wave would probably not seriously disrupt it, although a train of such higher waves might.

While precise data are not available it would seem that some sea walls have withstood the test of time with aprons of thickness of the order of one sixth the off-shore wave height, or on steep slopes one tenth to one twelfth the breaking wave height. Therefore if the liberal approach referred to gives a thickness that the designer considers somewhat excessive in the circumstances, there is usually scope for reduction based upon knowledge of existing aprons in the vicinity, which have withstood similar conditions successfully. (For the detailed design of aprons that are required also to release hydrostatic pressures, see Section 3.4.)

A recent investigation[9] of plunging waves breaking on plain rectangular blocks placed on a 2:1 impermeable surface, with gaps between and under the blocks showed the following results. The greatest uplift forces occurred at or slightly below the wave plunge area and slightly above the line of recession of the wave. Small gaps between the blocks caused a small reduction of uplift force in the plunge area, but some increase of uplift force in the area of wave recession. No clear relationship was found between the uplift forces and the wave heights and periods except that uplift force increased with wave height and to a lesser extent with increase in wave period, and increase in period increased the area affected. It appears that with short periods, uplift at the recession area was greatest, while with long periods uplift in the wave plunge area was greatest.

Uplift forces were found to be less with small gaps between the blocks and, particularly, less with small spaces under the blocks, the latter reducing uplift from both wave breaking and receding. The average uplift was found to be roughly half when the space under the blocks was reduced from 6% to 0.4% of the block size. Hence the Report recommends that the gaps under and between the blocks should generally be as small as practicable, but points out that in some circumstances it might be an advantage to have bigger gaps between and under the blocks in the wave recession line area. The tests supported the one sixth empirical design basis (for concrete).

4.13 INTERLOCKING CONCRETE BLOCKS

On walls where wave action is not severe, interlocking blocks provide a very satisfactory form of revetment and have the merit that they can be laid rapidly by unskilled labour.

Their chief advantages structurally are as follows. They are flexible, so that there is no risk of the apron arching over hollows and subsequently failing when exposed to wave attack. Subsidence is quickly noticed as the blocks flex, showing up the depressions, and if the subsidence is too great, the blocks can be quickly lifted and re-laid after the hollows have been filled. As the blocks are not jointed with mortar, hydrostatic pressures building up under the apron are released before any damage is done, and where they are used to give protection to the landward side of the wall, the apron is not impermeable and there is perhaps therefore less danger of desiccation of the underlying clay (for the design of interlocking blockwork revetments to release hydrostatic pressures, see Section 3.4).

The blocks are often used on estuary walls, and care has to be taken to ensure that they are not damaged by frost action resulting from alternate wetting and freezing. In tests to investigate this, blocks made from different concrete mixes were immersed in boiling water for long periods and subsequently subjected to alternate freezing and thawing. The results showed that blocks made of 1:2:4 concrete disintegrated after this treatment had been repeated a number of times, whereas 1:1½:3 concrete blocks made of well graded aggregate showed no deterioration whatsoever after 30 freezings when the experiment was discontinued. Following the tests, the mix adopted was 1 volume of cement to R volumes of fine aggregate to 3 volumes of coarse aggregate, R being the ratio of fine to coarse aggregate determined so that the combined aggregate lies within and nearer to the upper boundary of the grading envelope given by percentage finer than: 20 mm sieve, 100%; 10 mm sieve, 55–65%; 5 mm sieve 35–42%; BS sieve No. 7, 28–35%; BS sieve No. 14, 21–28%; BS sieve No. 25, 14–21%; BS sieve No. 52, 3–5%; BS sieve No. 100, 0%. The amount of water used is the absolute minimum necessary consistent with workability, and the moulds are vibrated a minimum 3000 impulses per minute. The minimum compressive strength

Fig. 44.   Kent type interlocking blocks being laid

after 28 days, using ordinary Portland cement, for cube tests is required to be 41.5 N/mm^2. The lower the water/cement ratio, the less water there is surplus to that needed for hydration. Consequently, the concrete contains fewer pores after the surplus water has evaporated and is therefore less porous, thereby reducing the extent to which water can be absorbed, freeze and cause spalling.

4.14   DESIGN OF KENT TYPE INTERLOCKING BLOCK APRONS

These blocks were introduced by the Kent Rivers Catchment Board in 1948 and have subsequently been referred to by some writers as shiplap blocks. They are made in sizes 380 mm × 380 mm × 200 mm thick and 150 mm thick, and are laid in courses breaking joint, often on a thin layer of very weak concrete. This blinding layer obviates the need to trim finely the clay face and provides a good surface on which to work. Details are given in Figs. 44 and 45. When laid in panels, the peripheral blocks are concreted in and where the areas of the panels are extensive or where the blocks are not laid in panels, some of the blocks are staked to the underlying clay by lengths of tubular steel driven through and grouted into holes left in the

139

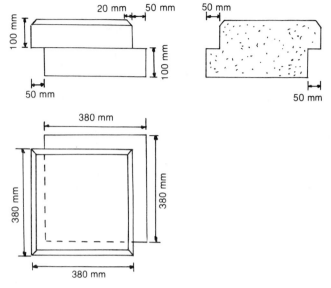

Fig. 45. Details of interlocking blocks

middle of special blocks. The spacing of the stakes depends on the degree of exposure to wave action.

A criticism sometimes made is that with settlement the blocks can tilt about a diagonal and foundation material can build up in the joints causing permanent displacement and perhaps ultimate failure. This view overlooks the fact that the normal practice is to lay the blocks on a layer of weak blinding concrete and hence foundation material is prevented from getting into the joints.

The wave heights resisted by the 200 mm thick blocks under various conditions of laying are set out in detail in Section 4.6.

It will have been seen in Section 4.12 that the resistance of blocks to wave action is roughly proportional to their thickness. The resistance of blocks of thickness greater or less than 200 mm can therefore be roughly assessed on this proportional basis from the data given in Section 4.6. For major schemes, it would be prudent to assess first the likely requirements by these means and then to confirm the conclusions by model tests reproducing the design conditions and the proposed panelling and panel perimeter conditions (see reference 10 for details of model tests).

140

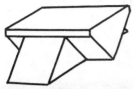

*Fig. 46.   Hydraulics research station
'W' type interlock block*

*Fig. 47.   'W' blocks being placed in connection with field trials of several forms
of interlocking revetment blocks being conducted by arrangement with the
Department of Engineering Services, Metropolitan Borough of Wirral*

4.15   DESIGN OF W–TYPE INTERLOCKING BLOCK APRONS

The Hydraulics Research Station interlocking block
aprons[11], evolved from work by A. F. Whillock are shown in
Figs. 46 and 47 which show them being placed in position in
test bays on the Wirral Peninsula, near Liverpool. For safe
design on steep slopes (not defined, but thought to be slopes of
4:1 or steeper) the Report recommends that the block thickness
should not be less than one sixth of the breaking wave height
(related to the design significant wave height), but considers
that on flat slopes the Wallingford block assembly should
remain intact with the breaking wave up to about ten times the
block thickness.

The relationship between block movement and wave period

is not clear, but it seems that the longer the wave period, the greater the block movement for the same height of wave.

The tests revealed that close fitting blocks on an impermeable foundation are more stable than those placed on a porous filter layer.

The Report recommends that movement of underlying material through the joints can be prevented by laying the blocks on a filter layer of coarser material or by using a woven plastic membrane.

4.16   OTHER TYPES OF INTERLOCKING BLOCKS

Proprietary interlocking blocks are available and the manufacturers usually give some guidance on how to arrive at a preliminary assessment of the size of block required. One maker suggests the use of the Hudson formula (see Section 4.26) with a K_D value of 60, but this advice is for guidance only and they stress that responsibility for the design in which their product is used is solely that of the purchaser.

A simpler approach is to base the initial design on the empirical one sixth the breaking wave height rule (see Sections 4.12 and 4.15).

Whatever methods are used for the preliminary assessments, for major schemes using (*all* types of) interlocking blocks, it will usually be prudent to carry out model tests reproducing the proposed panelling, panel perimeter conditions, tide levels and corresponding sea states to be expected under the design return period conditions.

4.17   ASPHALT AND ASPHALT PAVING

Asphalt is a mixture of bitumen and inert mineral matter (to avoid confusion, it should be noted that bitumen is referred to as asphalt in America), the latter, in sea defence work, usually consisting of one or more of the following: sand (passing 10 mesh sieve but retained on 200 mesh sieve), coarse aggregate, filler (minimum 70% passing 200 mesh sieve), asbestos fibres (used to increase the property of the asphalt to remain in place and not flow on slopes).

Asphalt is flexible, durable and ductile (giving resistance to

142

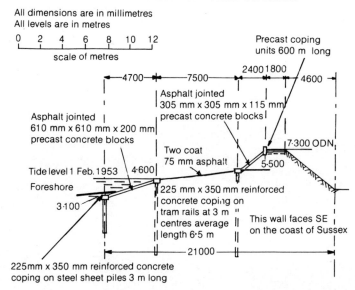

All dimensions are in millimetres
All levels are in metres

0 2 4 6 8 10 12
scale of metres

Precast coping
units 600 m long

2400 1800

←4700→ ←7500→ 4600

Asphalt jointed
305 mm x 305 mm x 115 mm
precast concrete blocks

Asphalt jointed
610 mm x 610 mm x 200 mm
precast concrete blocks

Two coat
75 mm asphalt

7·300 ODN

Tide level 1 Feb. 1953   4·600

5·500

Foreshore

3·100

225 mm x 350 mm reinforced
concrete coping on
tram rails at 3 m
centres average
length 6·5 m

This wall faces SE
on the coast of Sussex

←21000→

225mm x 350 mm reinforced concrete
coping on steel sheet piles 3 m long

The tide level of 1 Feb. 1953 coincided with the surge in the North Sea so that
on the south coast this tide was accompanied by an offshore wind. With onshore
winds extra. HWST level is 4·000, MHWST is 3·400, MLWST is − 3·300

Fig. 48. Details of Pett sea wall

impact). If required it can be made impervious and it is not
affected chemically by sea water. Within limits the proportions
of the different materials can be varied according to the qualities required.

It must be borne in mind, however, that the specific gravity
of bitumen is approximately 1 and in consequence asphalt is
very much lighter than concrete. Under water, asphalt has
only about 75% of the weight of concrete and therefore
wherever it is used, care must be taken to prevent the development of hydrostatic pressure under the apron.

The berm of the Pett sea wall (slope 8:1, horizontal to vertical) is an example of the use of asphalt in sea defence work (see
Figs. 48 and 49 and Chapter 5) and consists of a two-coat
paving laid on shingle. The shingle was sprayed with bituminous emulsion and covered with 25 mm of asphalt, and hand-
tamped in strips. On this a 50 mm top coat was laid and
consolidated by a 2.5 tonne roller. Because of the shingle foundation, the asphalt was made very flexible by the use of high

Fig. 49.   Pett sea wall

penetration bitumen. Its composition was: base course, 75% sand, 10% limestone filler, 15% bitumen 180/200 penetration; top course, 72% sand, 15% limestone filler, 13% bitumen 180/200 penetration. A drainage system was provided to prevent failure by uplift pressure.

When the foundation is clay, care must be taken to clear all growth and spray with weed killer before the asphalt is laid.

If paving is to be used on a wall facing south, due regard must be paid to this in deciding the composition of the asphalt, since during the summer months, the intensity of the sun's rays on it will be greater than would be the case if it faced north. Only flat slopes would be advisable under such conditions, together with the use of low penetration bitumen. In assessing the possibilities of different types of revetment, it should not be forgotten that emergency repairs to asphalt under storm conditions are more difficult than to other types of facings.

Other applications of asphalt in sea defence and coast protection works are given in Sections 3.5 and 4.18.

144

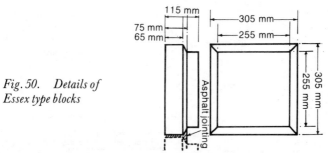

*Fig. 50. Details of
Essex type blocks*

4.18   TYPES OF ASPHALT JOINTED CONCRETE BLOCKS

For estuary walls and for sea walls where wave action is not too great, the Essex type block (Fig. 50) has been widely used. Those on the bottom slope of the Pett sea wall (see Figs. 48 and 49 and Chapter 5) are 610 mm × 610 mm × 200 mm thick. In Essex, blocks for estuary walls are usually 380 mm × 380 mm × 125 mm, but where heavier wave action is expected, as at Tendring, a 305 mm cube is employed.

In the foregoing cases, the jointing compound formula was, by weight, 47% bitumen, 47% sand and 6% asbestos fibres. The bitumen penetration varied from 15/25 to 40/50. In comparing blocks of this type with interlocking blocks, it should be remembered that if they have to be relaid, it is necessary to clean off the asphalt jointing and that under convex flexing (at the perimeter of a subsided area for example) they are likely to be less strong. A further disadvantage is the difficulty of satisfactory repair work being carried out under bad winter conditions.

For exposure to severe wave action, an even heavier block is needed, and Figs. 51 and 67 illustrate the 380 mm cube blocks used on the Northern Sea Wall from Reculver to Birchington in Kent (see Chapter 5). The lower part of the joint is filled with pure bitumen and the upper part with a compound of the proportions by weight, bitumen 47%, sand 47% and asbestos fibres 6%, the sand being ⅛ in (3.3 mm) down approved grading, the asbestos 2–4 mm fibres, the bitumen being 20/30 penetration on the 3 : 1 slope (horizontal to vertical) and 40/50 penetration on the 5 : 1 slope. The concrete used in the blocks is in accordance with the specification given in Section 4.13 for interlocking blocks.

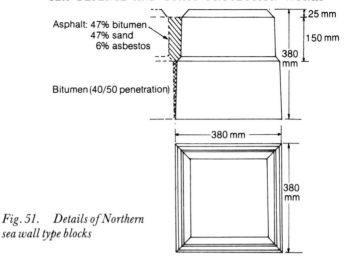

Asphalt: 47% bitumen
47% sand
6% asbestos

Bitumen (40/50 penetration)

25 mm

150 mm

380
mm

380 mm

380
mm

*Fig. 51. Details of Northern
sea wall type blocks*

The sides of the blocks are primed before placing and when necessary the joints are dried by flame gun before the jointing is poured. On the lowest part of the Northern Sea Wall apron, where settlement could not occur and where it would have been impossible to dry the joints completely, the blocks were grouted in 1 : 3 cement/sand mortar with, as required, sufficient quick-setting additive.

On steep slopes there is a tendency for asphalt jointing to run, so that maintenance works are required. In the Authors' experience, 3 : 1 should be regarded as the maximum slope desirable.

In particular cases it is possible to consider the possibility of adding rubber to the bitumen (in the proportion of about 5% of the bitumen content) in order to increase the flexibility of the asphaltic jointing. The addition of rubber reduces the penetration of the bitumen so that with it a bitumen one grade lighter could usually be used. Expert advice on this, as with all asphaltic compounds, should be sought from the petroleum firms who supply bitumen.

4.19   RELATIVE DURABILITIES OF VARIOUS FACINGS

In connection with the Dymchurch sea wall reconstruction scheme, the following durability tests were carried out. Blocks

146

of granite, concrete and ragstone were, in turn, held stationary in a rotary drum concrete mixer containing shingle, sand and water. The drum was rotated as for mixing concrete. The abrasive material, carried to the top of the drum, fell on to the surface of the block and rolled down the face, producing an action very similar to natural conditions of sea wall abrasion on shingle and sand foreshores. Each block was kept in the mixer for ten hours. At the end of the tests, the surfaces were similar in appearance to those of naturally abraded sea wall facing blocks. The blocks were weighed before and after testing and the percentage loss of weight for each was recorded.

The relative durabilities were found to be: granite blockwork, 1; concrete blockwork (to the specification given in Section 4.13, age at least nine months) 0.26; ragstone blockwork, 0.24. The tests were devised and carried out by J. Evans, Consulting Engineer.

The comparative costs for the facings per unit area were: Swedish granite, 1.0; concrete, 0.8; ragstone, 0.68; so that the relative costs per unit area for the life period of the granite were: granite, 1.0; concrete, 2.67; ragstone, 2.85. Ragstone 300 mm thick laid at the seaward toe of the Dymchurch sea wall towards the end of the last century had a useful life of about fifty years, so that under the same conditions of sand and shingle abrasion, 380 mm granite blocks should last 250 years and 380 mm concrete blocks, 68 years.

In situ concrete may be expected to have a shorter life than that of pre-cast blocks since the blocks can (*a*) be cast face downwards for added compaction on the face, (*b*) be cast with a smaller water/cement ratio, giving greater strength, (*c*) be vibrated better and (*d*) are not subject to wave action when setting. Hence, where considerable abrasion is expected, pre-cast blocks are normally used rather than in situ concrete.

4.20 REINFORCED CONCRETE PANEL WALLS AND WAVE WALLS

On exposed walls the need for constructing blockwork in panels to give, in some cases, greater resistance to wave action and in all cases to limit the area of damage in the event of a wash-out, has already been mentioned. The panel walls are commonly of reinforced concrete.

Table 4.1 Vibrated concrete

Aggregate sieve size	20 mm aggregate; percentage passing (by weight)	40 mm aggregate; percentage passing (by weight)
40 mm mesh	100	100
20 mm mesh	100	59–67
10 mm mesh	55–65	44–52
5 mm mesh	35–42	32–40
BS Sieve No. 7	28–35	25–31
BS Sieve No. 14	21–28	17–24
BS Sieve No. 25	14–21	12–17
BS Sieve No. 52	3–5	7–11
BS Sieve No. 100	0–3	0–2

Mix: maximum aggregate size 40 mm or 20 mm, limits of aggregate/cement ratio by weight, maximum 5.5, minimum 3.5, minimum crushing strength within 28 days, 40 N/mm^2.

Cover to bars should preferably be at least 75 mm and considerably more where severe abrasion is expected.

The upper part of the Northern Sea Wall revetment (Fig. 66) is a typical example of this kind of construction. The box-type units are constructed with expansion joints transversely to accommodate contraction and differential settlement between the adjoining units. To allow for settlement down the slope, the units are joined together with hinge joints (for settlement, see Chapter 3). The expansion joints are of normal design (that is they are filled with expansion joint material, primed and sealed with sealing compound) and the hinge joints consist of expansion joint material and steel bars or flats wrapped in Densotape or otherwise protected against corrosion, the whole so constructed that a hinge is formed and the revetment given a high degree of flexibility.

The individual units (that is, boxes) forming the panels are designed so that in the event of a wash-out, whatever the means of support of the unit, the stress in the reinforcing steel is below yield point; the amount by which the stress under these conditions is below yield point depending on the degree of likelihood of the unit ever having to be so supported.

Wave walls which usually form part of the upper portion of the panelling, are designed with conservative working stresses to withstand the wave pressures exerted on them (see Section 1.20) and lateral loads caused by traffic along the crest of the wall.

An alternative approach to the design of the reinforced concrete that can now be used is that of limit state design. An account of the use of this method[12] applicable to sea defence works is given in Draft BSI Code of Practice on Maritime Structures Part 1.

To ensure satisfactory resistance to sulphate attack, frost action and abrasion, for sea walls, vibrated concrete as shown in Table 4.1 has been found satisfactory in Kent.

4.21 SHEET PILING

Timber and steel sheet piles are used mainly as toe walls to protect sea walls from failure by scour at the toe at times when the foreshore has been lowered by storms. They are also used as panel cut-off walls to contain blockwork at low levels on the foreshore where construction in in situ concrete would be unduly difficult and expensive. Fig. 66 illustrates both these uses.

4.22 SUB-APRON GROUTING

It sometimes happens that hollows form under an old sea wall revetment, rendering it liable to destruction by heavy wave action. One possible remedy is to pump aerated grout under the apron. This was done with success on the Dymchurch sea wall where hollows had developed between the stonework and the underlying poor quality earthen wall. The equipment comprised a combined mixer and pump, grouting pump and flexible hose.

After experiments, the following procedure was adopted. Holes were drilled in the apron at two metre centres, alternate rows being staggered, and 25 mm standpipes were caulked into them. Aerated grout in the proportions of 25 kg cement to 76 kg sand to 0.3 litre Teepol and 14 litre water was then pumped through the standpipes, commencing on the lower part of the apron and proceeding up the slope.

The usual working pressure at the pump was between 1.40

and $1.75 \, \text{kg/cm}^2$ and was not allowed to exceed $5.25 \, \text{kg/cm}^2$. The sand conformed to the following grading (percentage by weight passing): 5 mm sieve, 100%; BS sieve No. 10, 70–100%; BS sieve No. 14, 60–100%; BS sieve No. 25, 30–100%; BS sieve No. 44, 11–72%; BS sieve No. 52, 5–64%; BS sieve No. 85, 2–40%; BS sieve No. 100, 0–14%.

Frequently, water and air were forced up through porous parts of the apron and this was found to be an indication of the path of the grout before it emerged from an adjoining standpipe. Rising pressures indicated that the ultimate acceptance had been reached. Second and third pressure build-ups were tried in each case and if on the third occasion the pressure immediately reached the maximum, the grouting at the particular point was considered complete. The standpipe and the adjoining ones from which grout had emerged were then capped.

Samples were taken of the grout emerging from the standpipes, from the mixer and from the pump, and these showed that the grout retained its aerated form after pumping and after travelling under the apron. After removal of the standpipes, the holes in the apron were sealed with a cement/sand mix to which quick-setting compound had been added.

The average acceptance of aerated grout per hole was $0.14 \, \text{m}^3$, the maximum acceptance at a hole was $1.70 \, \text{m}^3$ and the average thickness of the grout under the apron was 50 mm.

Three inspection holes were broken out in the apron. They revealed no voids and at one hole the grout was found to have filled completely what had evidently been a void 100–150 mm in depth and 200–250 mm in width. It had also penetrated well into the lower parts of the blockwork joints.

4.23   PERMEABLE SEA WALLS

Walls made of armour units are permeable and the importance of this is explained in Chapter 2. Walls built of them can be given steep slopes thereby saving material, and their roughness is such that the swash height is less than for a smooth wall of the same slope. Their design is discussed in Section 4.26. Their use is mainly confined to harbour works, but on lengths of coast where amenity aspects, access for the public and the likelihood of children crawling into the interior of the wall do not need to be considered, there is scope under some conditions for the design of sea walls incorporating these blocks which are generally superior to rectangular blocks laid pell-mell. Tetrapods weighing about 4 Mg each, were used in strengthening the Marine Drive sea wall, Bombay.

Another form of permeable longitudinal sea defence used on the East coast of England for toe-of-cliff protection comprises a timber cribwork filled with concrete blocks or large stones and this can be built in conjunction with a system of groynes.

4.24 WAVE SCREENS

Fig. 52 shows the wave screen that was built on the Pett foreshore, Sussex. Wave screens are another form of permeable longitudinal sea defence work and usually consist of timber piles driven well into the shingle with spaces between them about equal to their width. The tops of those at Pett were constructed at the level of high water spring tide. They are generally built in conjunction with other sea defence works; in this case, in conjunction with a timber (box type) barrier filled with shingle farther up the beach on the landward side of the screen and with a system of groynes. Their function is to reduce the energy of the waves.

Fig. 52.   Pett wave screen, timber barrier and permeable groyne

For the system of sea defence described to be successful, adequate shingle feed is required. At the present time a design of this kind would not generally be considered economical in England and the cheaper alternative would often be a beach recharge scheme (see Section 2.7).

4.25 DESIGN OF RIPRAP REVETMENTS

This Section sets out to provide the designer with a simple example for the provision of a riprap revetment. The design is based upon CIRIA Report[13] Number 61, to which the reader is referred for full details. Fig. 53 shows a section of the site to which protection is to be provided. The hydraulic conditions of the site are a maximum still water level of 3.5 m AOD, a significant wave height H_s of 2 m and a significant wave period P_s of 6.5 s.

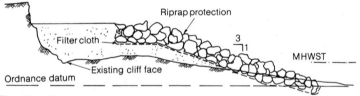

Fig. 53. Riprap revetment

Step one is to determine the relationship between the significant wave height H_s and the significant wave height defined by the zero down crossings $\bar{H}_s$. In this case H_s is approximated to $\bar{H}_s$.

Step two determines the relationship between the significant period P_s and the mean zero crossing wave period $\bar{P}_r$.

$$\bar{P}_r = 0.91 P_s = 0.91 \, (6.5) = 5.92 \, s$$

Step three allows for the determination of maximum run-up $\bar{r}_u{}^m$ and run-down $\bar{r}_d{}^m$.

For 2 : 1 and 3 : 1 slopes $\bar{r}_u{}^m = 2.0\bar{H}_s$
For 4 : 1 slopes $\bar{r}_u{}^m = 1.25\bar{H}_s$
For 6 : 1 slopes $\bar{r}_u{}^m = 0.92 \, \bar{H}_s$
For all slopes $\bar{r}_d{}^m = 0.14 \, \bar{P}_r \left(g \, \bar{H}_s\right)^{1/2} \tan \alpha$

where α is the angle of the riprap slope.

152

Assuming a 3 : 1 slope

$$\text{run-up } \bar{r}_u^m = 2.0 \, \bar{H}_s = 2.0 \, (2.0) = 4 \, \text{m}$$

This run-up must be added to the still water level to determine the maximum crest level to which the riprap should be provided. Therefore, maximum crest height becomes

$$\text{still water level} + \bar{r}_u^m = 3.5 \, \text{m AOD} + 4 \, \text{m} = 7.5 \, \text{m AOD}$$

Run-down can be determined by using the formulae provided and deducting the value from still water level. Step four requires the determination of the median rock diameter D^R_{50}. For the purpose of this example it has been assumed that an intermediate damage criterion is acceptable, that criterion B applies. The mean number of waves attacking the structure during a storm is calculated as follows. From the design tide curve, wave action acts for a period of two hours, approximately 7000 seconds.

$$\bar{P}_r = 5.92 \, \text{s}$$

Therefore

$$\text{mean number of waves} = 7000/5.92 = 1182$$

Reference to Fig. 54 applying to criterion B gives a design value

$$\bar{H}_s/D^R_{50} = \delta = 2.2$$

Transposing $\bar{H}_s/D^R_{50} = 2.2$, given $\bar{H}_s = 2.0 \, \text{m}$, gives

$$D^R_{50} = 2/2.2 = 0.91 \, \text{m}$$

This may be converted into a block size assuming a stone having a density of $2700 \, \text{kg/m}^3$. The weight of a median block D^R_{50} may be obtained as follows.

$$\text{weight of median block} = \pi \times \frac{0.91^3}{6} \times 2700 = 1065 \, \text{kg}$$

The maximum riprap block D^R_{85} may be obtained from the relationship

$$D^R_{85}/D^R_{50} = 1.5$$

That is

$$D^R_{85} = 1.50 \times D^R_{50} = 7.50 \times 0.91 = 1.37 \, \text{m}$$

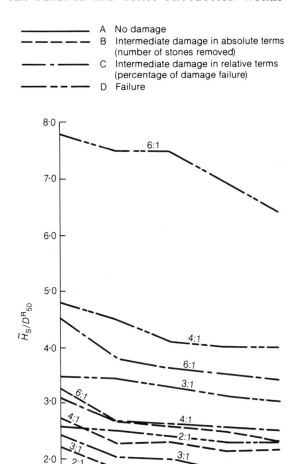

A No damage
B Intermediate damage in absolute terms
   (number of stones removed)
C Intermediate damage in relative terms
   (percentage of damage failure)
D Failure

Fig. 54.   Riprap design chart (data taken from Fig. 20 of CIRIA report 61, reproduced by permission of the Director of CIRIA)

154

The weight of a maximum block D^R_{85} may be obtained as follows.

$$\text{weight of maximum block} = \frac{\pi \times 1.37^3}{6} \times 2700 = 3630\,\text{kg}$$

Similarly the minimum block size D^R_{15} may be obtained from

$$D^R_{15}/D^R_{50} = 0.67$$

Hence

$$D^R_{15} = 0.67\,D^R_{50} = 0.67 \times 0.91 = 0.61\,\text{m}$$

The weight of the minimum block D^R_{15} may be obtained as follows.

$$\text{weight of minimum block} = \frac{\pi \times 0.61^3}{6} \times 2700 = 320\,\text{kg}$$

Step five is to calculate the thickness to which the riprap is to be provided. CIRIA draws attention to the fact that if the designer has adopted the two criteria (C and D in Fig. 54) which are based on failure, the riprap thickness of $2D^R_{50}$ should be adopted. In the cases of no damage a reduced thickness may be adopted.

Step six requires the determination of the filter materials from the following relationships.

Maximum filter material diameter $D^F_{85} \leqslant D^R_{85}/4$

Median filter material diameter $D^F_{50} \leqslant D^R_{50}/7$

Minimum filter material diameter $D^F_{15} \leqslant D^R_{15}/7$

In the case of a maximum block D^R_{85} of unit weight less than 5000 kg, an alternative the designer may wish to consider is the replacement of the filter material by a nylon filter fabric cloth.

Step seven is the calculation of the filter thickness. CIRIA Report 61 gives the advice that the minimum thickness should not be less than $0.5D^R_{50}$.

Section 6.4 gives further information about riprap, including comparison of the damage history of prototype riprap with that estimated in accordance with Report 61.

4.26 DESIGN OF ARMOUR UNIT WALLS

The use of armour units, such as the tetrapod (French, see Fig. 71) in coast protection work has been referred to in Section 4.23. The tetrapod is believed to be the first complex armour unit (as distinct from concrete cube or rectangular blocks) to have been developed. Others include the stabit (British, see Fig. 71), quadripod (American), dolos (South African) and tri-bar (American).

Work at the US Army Engineer Waterways Experiment Station[14] produced the well-known Hudson equation for the stability of quarry stone cover layers to rubble-mound break-waters when the crest of the structure is high enough to prevent major overtopping and with slopes not steeper than 1.5 : 1. Later, the expression was extensively extended in coastal engineering practice to cover armour units. The equation is

$$W = \frac{w_r H^3}{K_D(S_r - 1) \cot \theta}$$

where W is the weight of the individual armour unit; w_r is the unit weight (saturated surface dry) of the armour unit; H is the design (significant) wave height; S_r is the specific gravity of the armour unit; and θ is the angle of structure slope measured from the horizontal. K_D varies with the shape, degree of inter-locking and other characteristics of the particular armour unit being used. Values for K_D for different types of units and also graphs can be obtained[15] to facilitate working out the Hudson expression.

For two layers of tetrapods, for example, for breaking waves, for the structure trunk, a K_D value of 7.2 is suggested. For the structure head (the upper part that suffers most wave attack) the value varies from 4.0 for slope of 3:1 to 5.9 for slope of 1.5:1.

These are no-damage criteria, but actually consider up to 5% damage. Values of K_D as a function of percentage damage are also given in the Shore Protection Manual,[15] together with detailed advice on the design of the underlayers, for example, for armour units with $K_D \leq 12$, the first underlayer quarry stone should weigh about $W/10$, the second underlayer stone about $W/200$, both layers minimum two stones thick, all laid

156

on a bedding/filter layer (see Section 3.4).

It will be seen that the Hudson equation does not take into account the wave period or the obliquity of the waves. Further, the design approach referred to is based on experiments using waves of uniform height. Recent investigations by the Hydraulics Research Station, Wallingford, and other research institutions, show that structures respond differently when exposed to different wave patterns. While this design approach is useful for preparing preliminary proposals, it is important that designs for major schemes should generally be model tested using irregular waves. The obliquity, occurrence and frequency of characteristic wave patterns, and, more rarely, possibility of multi-directional waves, for the particular site should be studied and where necessary incorporated in the model test. This latter approach is particularly important in the case of blocks whose stability depends materially on their interlocking characteristics.

Model experiments appear to indicate that complex armour units are likely to be more affected by increase in wave period than natural stone blocks; also that when armour units with a high degree of interlocking fail, they fail extensively, whereas damage tends to become progressively severe in the case of stone blocks or armour units with less interlocking. These are factors to take into account when designing armour unit revetments. Care must also be taken to ensure that the units are structurally adequate for placing and for their purpose. It is likely that reinforcement will often not be found necessary for blocks weighing under 15 tonnes. Reinforcement naturally adds very considerably to the cost.

It would seem that generally stone block revetments are more stable under oblique waves than when the direction of wave approach is normal to the wall, but this may not necessarily be true of armour units; hence the advisability of taking into account the angle or angles of wave approach when designing armour unit protective works (another useful reference on the stability of armour units is reference 16).

4.27   COST/BENEFIT STUDIES

Often, for cost/benefit studies, the procedure is to select a range of return periods and for each of these to estimate the cost of the most effective works to give those degrees of protection and the associated capitalised benefits. By 'most effective works' is meant considering alternative ways of achieving the same result, in order to find the cheapest that is both effective and acceptable. This is cost effectiveness and not, in itself, cost/benefit.

If curves are then plotted with return period on the x-axis and cost and capitalised benefit on the y-axis, and then if the benefit curve is generally above the cost curve, there will be a return period for which the difference between benefit and cost is greatest. This would be the return period to adopt if the biggest return possible on the scheme was desired.

The next aspect to study is the value of benefit/cost ratios for various return periods. These can be calculated from the two curves and plotted as a third curve. It will often be found that the return period with the highest value of benefit/cost ratio is different from that giving the highest return, and the return period corresponding to the highest benefit/cost ratio is, of course, that corresponding to the scheme that gives the greatest value per £1 of cost.

There is the further consideration that it is often possible to greatly increase the standard of protection, in terms of increased return period standard, at the cost of only a very modest percentage increase in cost. The difficulty here is that for sea defence schemes, increase in benefit at the upper end of the scale is often very insensitive to relatively large increases in return period. For example, a third of a metre rise in tide level, at the higher levels, can often mean a very considerable increase in return period. On the other hand, the increase in cost, although modest in terms of percentage increase on the total cost, is often not matched by a favourably larger benefit increment, even though the total capitalised benefit is still greater than the total estimated cost.

Sometimes yet a further somewhat similar consideration occurs. Referring to Fig. 55, it could be that for a peninsula, alternative schemes are considered, the first providing a wall from A to C and C to E to protect the area ACE and the second a scheme providing a wall along AB, BD and DE to protect the area ABDE.

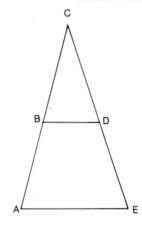

Fig. 55. Diagrammatic representation of alternative schemes for the protection of a peninsular

The studies could show that both schemes were economically viable and that scheme AB, BD, DE was estimated to cost £1.75m and scheme ACE £3.75 m. The problem is to decide which scheme to adopt.

One approach in times of financial stringency would be to say, comparing the two schemes, it is costing £2m more to protect the area BCD over and above that to protect area ABDE, but the benefit provided for BCD is much less than £2m and therefore the provision of the walls BC and CD cannot be justified.

The foregoing illustrates the self-evident fact that cost/benefit studies are simply aids to decision making (see also reference 17).

4.28 BENEFITS FROM SEA DEFENCE WORKS

For an urban/industrial area it is necessary first to compile a list of the types of property where damage will be avoided or reduced by the scheme. The list would usually include domestic property, offices, shops, factories, warehouses, roads, vehicles, railways and public utilities.

Next an assessment is made of the value of damage likely to be done by various depths of flooding. Questionnaires can be sent to the main factories and to representative shops, offices, and so on asking for estimates of damage to buildings, stock, equipment and loss of trading profit. For domestic properties, values can be taken from known value of damage for similar flood levels for similar properties, or, as a rough evaluation, for ground floor flooding only, 10% of the value of the properties.

In the case of roads, apart from the value of physical damage, there is the value of traffic delays. The Department of the Environment have available assessments for the latter related to factors such as lost working time. Local highway departments can usually provide present and expected vehicle flows. On trunk roads the proportion of vehicles is probably of the order of 78% cars, 20% goods vehicles and 2% public transport. In addition, there are the costs of emergency services, fire, police and social services.

In the case of rural areas, for minor schemes, it is possible to compare the cost per hectare of the scheme with the market value per hectare of the land that would be protected and from this to determine the viability or otherwise of the proposals.

For more major schemes, more detailed studies are usually required. Increased protection from flooding means generally an increase in the annual gross margin and in the United Kingdom, agricultural economists at the Universities and the Agricultural Development Advisory Service of the Ministry of Agriculture, Fisheries and Food, will provide estimates of increased gross margin arising from the improved protection given by a scheme.

The annual gross margin is, per annum, the gross income less variable costs. Gross income is total income from the sale of the farm products. Variable costs are those arising from purchase of feeding stuffs, stock, seeds, fertilizers and casual labour. Fixed costs are those of permanent labour, machinery, maintenance and rent.

The increase in annual gross margin will not immediately follow the completion of the improvement scheme, but rather will increase as the farmers, gaining confidence in the improved protection, carry out land improvements, particularly land drainage improvements. Penning-Rowsell and Chatterton[18] found that resulting from a scheme in Kent, subsequent land drainage improvements extended over about 21 years, with a maximum rate at about the 7th year. The figures were as follows: after 5 years, 19%; 7 years, 54%; 10 years, 75%; 15 years, 92%.

In addition, there is value of damage by floods avoided to farm buildings, roads, machinery, crops, cattle, cost of reinstating the land following saline inundation and losses incurred during the period of reinstatement.

Also, to the benefits may be added the costs of sea wall reinstatement that would otherwise be incurred if the improvement were not carried out.

Finally there are the imponderables. These are losses that are very real, but are difficult to evaluate, such as distress, inconvenience, exposure, injury, death, loss of business or other opportunities. It is quite customary to add 50% to 100% to allow for these. Recently it has become more common to produce a net benefit/cost ratio and then in doubtful cases, where the benefit was less than the cost, to give weight to the imponderables, particularly risk to human life, to see if they justify proceeding with the scheme.

A great wealth of information is given by Penning-Rowsell and Chatterton,[18] on the techniques of cost/benefit studies, including the use of computers, together with very detailed data on damage costs for various types of properties, services, and so on. A further valuable reference by Penning-Rowsell is reference 19.

4.29   AVERAGE ANNUAL VALUE OF BENEFITS

Having determined the values of the damage that would arise for various depths of flooding, the next step is to relate areas and depths of flooding to return periods before and after improvement, and hence relate values of damage before and after improvement to return periods. This is based on the return periods of overtopping volumes obtained from the model tests for the wall before and after improvement and/or other considerations (such as when serious breaching was likely to occur and the areas and depths of flooding that could be expected to result from breaching).

Exceedence probability is defined as the reciprocal of the return period, that is, 1/return period. It is the probability that the event concerned will be equalled or exceeded in any one year.

Fig. 56 shows for a major scheme on the x-axis the exceed-

161

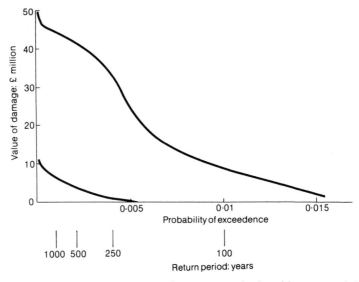

Fig. 56. Graphical determination of average annual value of damage avoided

ence probability of various occurrences plotted against, on the *y*-axis, the estimated total damage that would be caused by each occurrence, the upper curve applying to conditions before improvement and the lower curve after improvement. It can be shown[18, 20] that the area between the two curves represents the average annual value of damage that would be avoided by the carrying out of the scheme. If each sub-square represents 0.001 times £5 million, and there are 60 such squares in the area between the curves, then the area represents the average annual value of damage avoided by the scheme, and is £300 000.

Alternatively, the average annual value of damage avoided can be obtained by tabulation: Table 4.2. This could represent a simple flood wall scheme at the upper end of an estuary, designed to give protection up to the 250 year conditions, to a short length protecting industrial premises.

In Table 4.2 the figures in column 3 are successively the differences between the figures in column 2 for the 5 year and 10 year conditions, 10 year and 20 year conditions and so on. The figures in column 5 are successively half the sum of the figures in column 4 for the 5 year and 10 year conditions, 10 year and

162

Table 4.2. Average damage values

Return period	Exceedence probability	Probability of flood in interval	Damage	Mean damage in interval	Expected annual damage £
5	0.2		8330		
10	0.1	0.1	11920	10125	1012.5
50	0.02	0.08	26775	19347	1547.8
250	0.004	0.016	43750	35262	564.2
					3124.5

20 year conditions, and so on. The figures in column 6 are the product of the figures in column 3 and column 5.

For simplicity of illustration Table 4.2 goes from 50 year to 250 year return period. For an actual scheme it would be advisable to include representative return periods in the tabulation between these two. Also, if some overtopping and hence some damage is expected on the longer return periods even after improvement, then a similar tabulation should be carried out covering the situation after improvement. The difference between the total expected annual damage from the two tabulations will then be the annual average value of damage avoided by the proposed scheme.

4.30 CAPITALISATION OF ANNUAL BENEFITS (DISCOUNTING)

Having obtained the average annual value of damage avoided and of benefits accruing, it is necessary to calculate the present day total value of these annual values over the life of the scheme.

This can be obtained by using the following expressions. The present value of £1, n years hence, is $1/(1+r)^n$, where r is the discount rate per cent per annum. The present value of £1 per annum for n years is $(1/r)\{1-[1/(1+r)]^n\}$.

For more details of discounted cash flow methods, the reader is referred to *An Introduction to Engineering Economics*.[21] This book contains tables which give the present value of £1 per annum for n years discounted at r per cent per annum, for values of n from 1 to 60 and values of r up to 20. These greatly facilitate the calculations.

For schemes attracting Government grant aid in Britain, the discount rate is the United Kingdom Treasury rate, the Public Sector Test Rate. This varies, but at the time of writing it is

5%. It will be seen that a scheme can become viable or non-viable according to whether this percentage is lowered or raised. In a similar way, the present day estimated cost of the scheme, if carried out over a number of years, can be calculated. From the capitalised present day value of the benefit and the present day estimated cost of the scheme, the benefit/cost ratio may be calculated.

4.31 RANDOM SEQUENCE OF EVENTS BY COMPUTER SIMULATION

Clearly, if a major flood occurs early in the life of the works, the present day value of the damage avoided is greater than if the major flood occurs towards the end of the life of the works. An obvious criticism of the graphical and tabulation methods is that they average out the damage avoided.

One way of meeting this objection that has been devised is to obtain random sequences of events by computer simulation. Let us suppose that, say, the 400 year flood, because of its infrequency, has little effect on the present total value of damage avoided. For the computer the array then contains 400 elements, each representing a particular event and the damage associated with it. The once in 400 years event is represented only once in the 400 elements, whereas there will be more elements representing more frequent events.

A random number generator then selects particular events at random over the, say, 50 years life of the works and the damage avoided at each event is discounted to its present day value. This process can be repeated by the computer a selected number of times and the results given as a range of discounted benefits together with the mean value, the mean value usually being used for the cost/benefit study. However, this approach is open to the objection that if this exercise is carried out a very large number of times, then the result will be the same as that obtained by the graphical (or the tabulation) method, at very much less effort.

4.32 COST/BENEFIT ASPECTS OF COAST PROTECTION WORKS

For sea defence works, the Ministry of Agriculture, Fisheries and Food have indicated clearly to Water Authorities in informal documents[22] the types of cost/benefit studies they require to justify schemes for central government grants. The procedures set out in this chapter are in conformity with these requirements.

In the case of coast protection works, undoubtedly the Department of the Environment must apply cost/benefit considerations when examining schemes submitted for government grants, but their methods of doing this have not been made public. At the present time, the Department have commissioned the Local Government Operational Research Unit to draw up a framework for the economic evaluation of coast protection schemes and one hopes this Report may be made public.

Where considerable overtopping of coast protection works results in flooding of residential and industrial areas, the same cost/benefit approach as that for such areas protected by sea defence works, applies.

A different case is where a road or a railway runs along the coast and is protected by coast protection works that, because of age or other reasons, need to be replaced and/or improved. Here the cost of the scheme can be compared with the cost that would otherwise be involved in constructing the road or railway on a re-alignment where it would not require coast protection works to safeguard its existence.

Again, as a simple approach, in favourable circumstances, it would be possible to justify sand recharge schemes by assessing, on the one hand, the cost of the scheme plus the capitalised cost of maintenance replenishment, and on the other, the capitalised value of the losses to the community concerned which would result from the scheme not being carried out and a consequential decline in the numbers of holiday visitors.

The economic viability of coast protection works to prevent erosion of cliffs can often present a problem. In some circumstances the economic viability of the works can be fairly easily established. A typical example could be in relation to London Clay cliffs.

The ultimate natural stable slope of London Clay has been shown to be[23] between about 8° and 10° but by toe protection, cliff grading and drainage (see Chapter 6) it is possible to stabilise such cliffs at much steeper slopes.

165

If therefore, landward of the top of the cliffs, as sometimes happens, there is a large area of housing development, then it may often be possible to show that the value of the houses, roads and services, within the area affected by a slope of 10° from the toe of the cliffs is much greater than the cost of the coast protection cliff stabilisation works.

In another situation, in an area of erodible cliffs, with a discount rate of 5%, a £1 million coast protection scheme protecting a large residential area would certainly be worth considering if, in the absence of the works, two or three £30 000 houses a year on average over the life of the works would otherwise become uninhabitable due to coast erosion.

REFERENCES

1 HYDRAULICS RESEARCH STATION. *North Wales Coast Road, A55, Llandulas to Aber.*.Report EX 808. Wallingford, Hydraulics Research Station, 1978.

2 HYDRAULICS RESEARCH STATION. *Annual report, 1979.* Wallingford, Hydraulics Research Station, 1979.

3 HYDRAULICS RESEARCH STATION. *Fleetwood and Cleveleys Sea Defences—a Study of Return Periods for Overtopping Discharge Exceeded.* Report 871. Wallingford, Hydraulics Research Station, 1979.

4 DOVER A. R. and BEA R. G. Application of reliability methods to the design of coastal structures. *Coastal Structures.* New York, American Society of Civil Engineers, 1979.

5 PEARSON W. J. and MOSKOWITZ L. A proposed spectral form for fully developed wind seas based on the similarity theory of S. A. Kitsigorodskii. *J. Geophys. Res.*, 1964, Dec.

6 PRICE W. A. *Proc. 16th Int. Conf. Coastal Engineering, Hamburg*, 1978, 25–48.

7 HUDSPETH R. T. *et al.* Analyses of hinged wavemakers for random waves. *Proc. 16th Int. Conf. Coastal Engineering, Hamburg*, 1978.

8 HMSO. *Hydraulics Research.* London, HMSO, 1976.

9 WHILLOCK A. F. *The Stability of Revetment Blocks under Wave Attack.* Report IT 195. Wallingford, Hydraulics Research Station, 1980.

10 HYDRAULICS RESEARCH STATION. *Model Study of a Precast*

Block Protective Apron for the Beach at Penrhyn Bay. Report EX 462. Wallingford, Hydraulics Research Station, 1969.

11 WHILLOCK A. F. *The Wallingford Interlocked Revetment Block.* Report IT 164. Wallingford, Hydraulics Research Station, 1977.

12 BRITISH STANDARDS INSTITUTION. *Maritime Structures*, part I. London, British Standards Institution (in draft).

13 THOMPSON D. M. and SHUTTLER R. M. *Design of Riprap Slope Protection against Wind Waves.* Report 61. London, Construction Industry Research and Information Association, 1976.

14 US ARMY COASTAL ENGINEERING RESEARCH CENTER. *Shore Protection Manual*, 7.169. Washington, US Government, 1975.

15 US ARMY COASTAL ENGINEERING RESEARCH CENTER. *Shore Protection Manual*, Table 7–6, 7.170. Washington, US Government, 1975.

16 PRICE W. A. Static stability of rubble mound breakwaters. *Dock and Harbour Authority*, 1979, **60,** May, No. 702.

17 CHAMBERS D. N. and ROGERS K. C. *The Economics of Flood Alleviation.* Reading, Local Government Operational Research Unit, Royal Institute of Public Administration, 1973.

18 PENNING-ROWSELL E. C. and CHATTERTON J. B. *The Benefits of Flood Alleviation: a Manual of Assessment Technique.* Farnborough, Saxon House Studies, 1977.

19 PENNING-ROWSELL E. C. *The Effect of Salt Contamination on Flood Damage to Residential Properties.* Middlesex Polytechnic flood hazard research project. Enfield, Middlesex Polytechnic, 1978.

20 KUIPER E. *Water Resources Project Economics.* London, Butterworths, 1971.

21 INSTITUTION OF CIVIL ENGINEERS. *An Introduction to Engineering Economics.* London, Institution of Civil Engineers, 1969.

22 COLE G. *Cost-Benefit Analyses for Flood Protection and Land Drainage Projects.* London, Ministry of Agriculture, Fisheries and Food, 1973.

23 HUTCHINSON J. N. The free degradation of London Clay cliffs. *Proceedings of Geotechnical Congress, Oslo*, 1957, **1,** 113.

Chapter 5

Further examples of sea, estuary and tidal river walls

5.1 GENERAL

The examples given in this chapter are additional to and supplement those described elsewhere in this book. Their purpose is to illustrate further the practical application of design principles and details set out at length in other chapters. The accompanying descriptions are therefore brief, since explanations of particular principles or details have already been given. For details of the Standards referred to, see Section 3.14.

5.2 ESTUARY AND TIDAL RIVER WALLS

Since estuary and tidal river walls are usually protected by the limited fetch and by the saltings, the main need is to ensure that they are of adequate height, thickness and stability and that sufficient protection is afforded against the (usually) small wave action caused by high winds or by navigation.

Earthwork heightening is limited by soil mechanics considerations and if the maximum practicable heightening by this means is insufficient, or if buildings prevent the addition of further clay or other materials for heightening, then the desired level has usually to be achieved by the construction of a concrete wall or similar structure.

5.2.1 Typical tidal river wall

Fig. 57 shows a typical Standard B improvement where the desired level of one metre above the design tide level has been achieved by heightening and strengthening with clay, or with part chalk, ash, or suitable colliery waste filling from local sources. The access along the top of the wall will be noted.

168

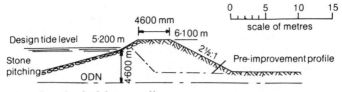

Fig. 57. *Details of tidal river wall*

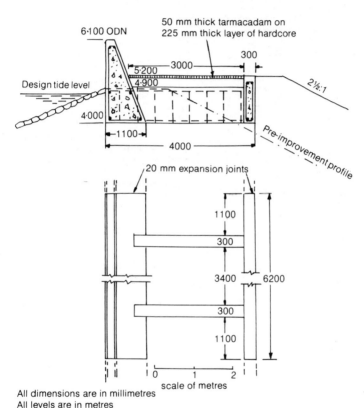

All dimensions are in millimetres
All levels are in metres

Fig. 58. *Details of tidal river crest wall*

If the soil mechanics investigations had indicated the likelihood of a considerable rate of settlement, then it would have been advisable to make the crest wider to enable the crest level to be raised periodically by 'topping up' and thus to defer as long as possible major raising and re-profiling at the stage when, by reason of 'topping up', the top width would no longer

169

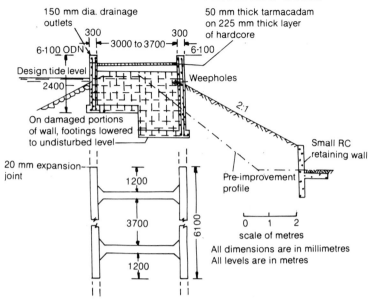

Fig. 59. Details of another type of tidal river crest wall

be adequate for access.

In the case illustrated, there was no need to provide a land-ward berm to prevent rotational or wedge failure following the raising of the crest, although this often has to be done (for details see Sections 3.6 to 3.8; for Standard A tidal walls, see also these Sections).

5.2.2 Tidal river wall heightening at restricted sites in industrial areas

Figs. 58 and 59 illustrate typical methods of raising, to Standard B, tidal river walls by the construction of reinforced concrete crest walls, where buildings on the landward side, or other structures, do not provide sufficient room for normal earthwork heightening.

5.2.3 Estuary wall

Fig. 60 shows a typical Standard B estuary wall. A top level of 6.1 m ODN was required on this length. The safe limit

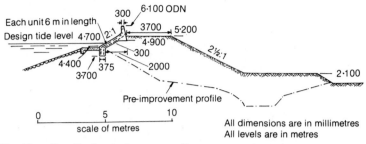

Fig. 60.   Details of typical estuary wall

for the top of the earthwork, even with the provision of a berm, was 5.2 m ODN so that the remaining 0.9 m raising was achieved by means of a reinforced concrete apron and wall which was designed to resist safely the stresses that develop as settlement of the newly placed clay takes place.

5.3   SEA WALLS FRONTED BY HIGH FORESHORES

Sea walls of this type are those where storm waves break on the foreshore before reaching the wall.

5.3.1 Seasalter sea wall

Fig. 61 shows the Standard B wall at Seasalter. Here a wide foreshore and shingle and shell deposits give good protection to the wall.

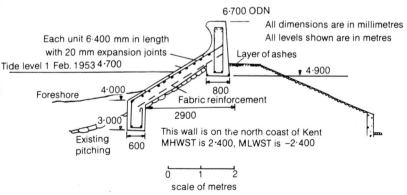

Fig. 61.   Details of Seasalter wall

171

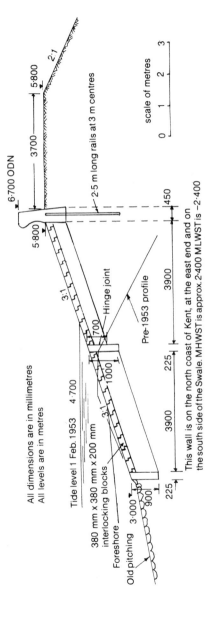

All dimensions are in millimetres
All levels are in metres

6·700 ODN

5·800

3700

2·1

5·800

2·5 m long rails at 3 m centres

450

3·1

Hinge joint

700

Pre-1953 profile

3900

1000

225

3900

3·1

Tide level 1 Feb. 1953   4·700

380 mm x 380 mm x 200 mm
interlocking blocks

Foreshore

Old pitching   3·000

900

225

This wall is on the north coast of Kent, at the east end and on
the south side of the Swale. MHWST is approx. 2·400 MLWST is −2·400

scale of metres

0   1   2   3

Fig. 62.   Details of Nagden sea wall

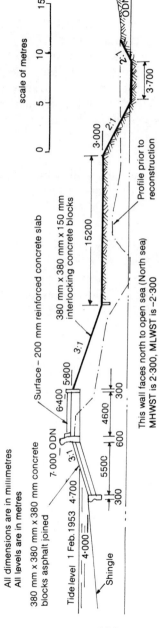

All dimensions are in millimetres
All levels are in metres

380 mm x 380 mm x 380 mm concrete
blocks asphalt joined

Surface – 200 mm reinforced concrete slab

380 mm x 380 mm x 150 mm
interlocking concrete blocks

7.000 ODN

Tide level 1 Feb. 1953   4·700

Shingle

Profile prior to
reconstruction

This wall faces north to open sea (North sea)
MHWST is 2·300, MLWST is –2·300

scale of metres

ODN

Fig. 63.   Details of Northern sea wall type T

173

5.3.2 Nagden sea wall

Fig. 62 gives details of the Standard B Nagden wall. The seaward revetment consists of a framework of reinforced concrete walls with a wave wall at the crest, each bay so formed being filled with 200 mm thick interlocking blocks. The connections between the upper and lower transverse walls are hinged (see Chapter 4) to allow for settlement of the placed clay on the landward side of the wall.

5.3.3 Pett sea wall

Figs. 48 and 49 show the Pett wall, which is to the west of Rye. This is an example of the use of bitumen in sea defence works and of a wide berm on the seaward revetment (see Chapter 4).

5.3.4 Northern sea wall type T

This wall, shown in Fig. 63, forms the crest unit of the main Northern Sea Wall Standard B design and has been constructed without further revetment where there is less exposure than on other lengths.

5.4 SEA WALLS FRONTED BY LOW FORESHORES

Sea walls of this type are those where the depth of water in front of the wall at high tide is so great that storm waves break on the wall itself. Fig. 37 illustrates this condition.

5.4.1 Dymchurch sea wall

Figure 38 shows details of this wall. Like the Pett sea wall, it is an example of a wall with a seaward berm. The conditions it has to withstand and model tests on it are described in Chapter 4. It comprises a heavy stone blockwork facing, mainly of ragstone, laid on a clay wall.

5.4.2 Sheerness sea wall

Model investigations carried out in connection with the design of this Standard A wall are described in Chapter 4. The

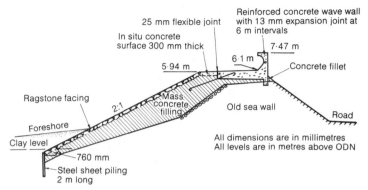

Fig. 64. Sheerness sea wall

Fig. 65. Sheerness sea wall

pre-improvement seaward apron varied in slope from 2:1 to 2.5:1.

It will have been seen from Section 4.3 that 2:1 is about the maximum slope for an apron to ensure that waves break on it (and are not reflected, causing severe disturbance of the foreshore) and therefore from Section 1.18 that maximum run-up and hence maximum overtopping can be expected with such a slope. The tests confirmed the belief that overtopping could be

175

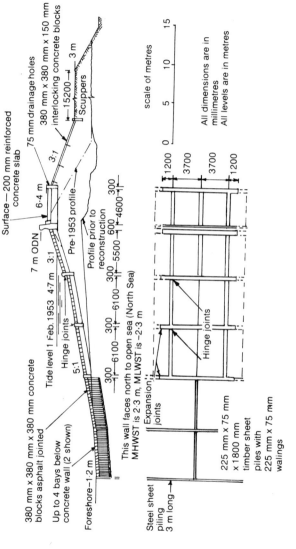

Fig. 66.   Details of Northern sea wall type V

176

*Fig. 67.   Northern sea wall type V, seaward face, showing 380 mm³ concrete
blocks set in asphalt jointing*

limited at much less cost by determining the best position, elevation and height for the wave wall, than by flattening the
seaward slope.

Circumstances were such that full advantage could be taken
of the benefits of placing the wave wall on the landward side of
the top of the main wall (see Section 4.4).

For a given top of main wall level, the investigations showed
that overtopping greatly decreased with heightening of the
wave wall. However for amenity reasons its height had to be
limited to 1.4 m and therefore the required reduction in overtopping had to be obtained by raising the level of the top of the
main wall while keeping on its landward side, the wave wall,
1.4 m high.

The wall is shown in Figs. 64 and 65. Three types of seaward
facing were employed: ragstone on mass concrete filling; in situ
concrete (when ragstone delivery rates were inadequate and
when timing considerations precluded the use of pre-cast
units); and a special design, described in Section 3.4, used over
a length where precautions had to be taken to prevent the development of hydrostatic pressures under the apron.

177

5.4.3 Northern sea wall type V

Figs. 66 and 67 show the main section of the Standard B Northern Sea Wall. The design of this wall is discussed in Chapter 4. The lower panels are formed with timber and steel sheet piling because of the difficulty of placing in situ concrete at the lower levels and because settlement was not expected at those levels.

Chapter 6

Special problems of coast protection works

6.1 COAST PROTECTION WORKS GENERALLY

Basically this book does not differentiate between sea defence works constructed under either of the enactments for the provision of sea defences in the United Kingdom, namely the Land Drainage Act 1976 and the Coast Protection Act 1949.

However, this chapter explores the particular requirements of coast protection works. Any sea defence scheme shares the basic design processes which are described in other chapters. Schemes designed within the Coast Protection Act involve additional facets of works which are particular to that Act, principally the inclusion of works to the land to the rear of defences where such works are necessary to guarantee stability of the defences. Fundamentally coast protection works comprise

(*a*) the prevention of encroachment and erosion by sea action, together with the prevention of any consequent flooding of land to the rear of the defences

(*b*) the stabilisation of the land to the rear of the defences if such stabilisation is needed to prevent the loss of the sea defences by movement of the land to their rear.

6.2 TOE PROTECTION BY SEA WALLS

The design process suitable for sea walls for cliff toe protection is set out in Chapter 4. The designer must ensure that the wall to be constructed does not encourage erosion. One simple rule to be applied is to dissipate wave energy horizontally, not vertically. Special care should be taken on soft foreshores where erosion can occur at the toe of the wall.

179

Fig. 68. Toe protection wall

One satisfactory type of wall takes the form of a sloping apron with two curved wave walls, one on the seaward and one on the landward side of a wide crest berm. An example of this type of wall is shown in Fig. 68. The toe of the apron is protected in this instance by a shingle beach. The apron has a gradient of 3 : 1 and is constructed using 200 mm thick interlocking concrete blocks laid upon a pea shingle drainage layer 100 mm thick. Bulk fill is laid under this construction and the loss of fines from this material is prevented by the use of a plastic filter fabric. The blocks are laid against a steel sheet pile toe wall capped with concrete and in situ or precast beams along the line of the groynes, the beams acting as a prop for the groyne, overcoming the need for raking support piles. The curved wave wall is one metre high based on Hydraulics Research Station recommendations, and has the dimensions in proportion to those given in Fig. 69.

With a profile of this kind a useful, if approximate, form of calculation can be used to determine the maximum height of rear wave wall required, where overtopping or protection of clay or friable cliffs are concerned. This is the addition of the design still water level and the significant wave height. In the case of chalk cliffs with chalk or chalk overlain by a thin layer of

180

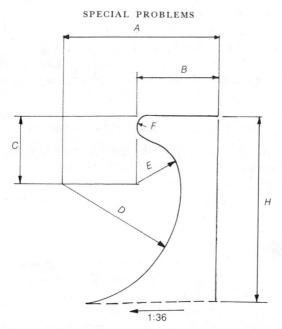

H	A	B	C	D	E	F
0·610	0·533	0·381	0·333	0·308	0·152	0·102
0·914	0·787	0·495	0·416	0·521	0·229	0·102
1·219	1·054	0·610	0·521	0·749	0·305	0·114
1·524	1·334	0·724	0·597	0·991	0·381	0·114
1·829	1·626	0·838	0·673	1·245	0·457	0·114

Fig. 69.   Dimensions of wave wall (metres)

sand foreshore, the level can usually be 0.5 m or so lower and
the wall slope correspondingly steeper. It must be emphasised
that to design any wall efficiently model testing must be
employed to evaluate the type of wall under construction.

Often the toe of the wall can be protected by beach. It is not
possible to generalise upon dimensions of such a beach, but if
beach profiles have been taken, as suggested in Section 1.21,
valuable guidance can be obtained as to likely crest heights,
beach gradients and drawdown.

Further reference to the design of beaches can be found in
Section 2.8. Proposed combinations of sea walls and beach sec-

tions can then be model tested under the various combinations of wave height and tide level corresponding to the design return period. The provision of a beach can have a major effect in controlling the hydraulic forces acting upon the defence.

6.3   TOE PROTECTION BY PERMEABLE REVETMENTS

In contrast to Section 6.2 the following sections describe sea defences which absorb energy within themselves in contrast to impermeable structures.

Many lengths of foreshore have a low financial and social value and when schemes are examined in a critical financial climate the cost of provision of traditional defences may exceed the benefits gained. The designer finds it difficult therefore to provide adequate forms of defence. Some forms of permeable defence, however, are cheap to provide and give the designer an opportunity to meet cost/benefit criteria.

Permeable sea defences take the form of aprons constructed in natural materials such as rock riprap or artifically constructed units such as tetrapods and stabits. Another alternative to an apron may be the use of rock or rubble-filled wire gabions or mattresses. In this country some works have been successfully completed using frames made of timber, timber and steel, or steel, forming a retaining structure for rock or rubble fill. The purpose of the rubble or rock fill is to provide additional energy absorption characteristics.

This latter form of construction has shown itself capable of having a life in excess of 20 years. Such defences are not totally free from maintenance and great care should be taken to replace any failed member, as such a failure can lead rapidly to destruction of the defences, caused by progressive and accelerating damage within the rubble fill of the revetment.

Fig. 53 shows a typical example of a rubble riprap scheme.

6.4   TOE PROTECTION BY RIPRAP

Many sea walls of necessity are large and expensive to construct. There is a need for the designer to examine his proposals against the general benefits likely to be gained by their con-

Fig. 70. Riprap

struction. This approach of cost/benefit has brought problems when only modest benefits are obtained by the construction of defences despite the obvious need for protection. It is these cost/benefit pressures that have brought about the re-evaluation of the rubble or rock riprap form of sea defence. It must be said that this form of construction provides protection at its simplest.

The Hydraulics Research Station was asked to research the principles of design of such a form of defence using random stone. This work culminated in a comprehensive report (reference 13, Chapter 4). This report was itself subjected to a further critical review in CIRIA Technical note 84[1]. The prototype studies were continued and the results of 2½ years of observations indicate that the design procedure of Report 61 may underestimate to some extent the size of riprap required (see Annual Report, CIRIA 80). A further method of design is outlined in the US Army Shore Protection Manual (reference 13, Chapter 1).

Riprap revetments are not water exclusive as is the case of monolithic sea walls. They gain their protection effectiveness by using their ability to absorb the wave energy within their structure.

Construction takes the form of the rock being placed on the site in a random manner within the grading calculated. The development of efficient filter fabrics allows riprap to be placed onto fill without the need to use a smaller stone filter, subject to the maximum weight of each block not exceeding 5000 kg, in which case a filter layer should be used.

When placing the riprap it is usual to have seaward facing slopes within the slope range of 2.5 : 1 to 4 : 1. Section 4.25 sets out a design example, and Fig. 70 shows a completed riprap wall provided to protect the flank of existing sea defences.

Where necessary, checks should be made to ensure failure by wedge or rotational slip will not occur.

6.5 TOE PROTECTION BY ARMOUR UNITS

In common with the riprap type of apron, toe protection can be achieved by the use of artificially constructed armour units instead of using a naturally occurring material. The units have a major advantage over the naturally occurring material in that within the available handling limits any size may be provided. They act in a similar manner to other forms of permeable defence in that they dissipate wave energy by turbulence and are secured in position by interlock and/or by interblock friction, as well as by their weight. This results in a higher stability coefficient which in turn permits the use of steeper structure side slopes or a lighter unit weight. Guidance on the design of armour units may be found in Section 4.26. Armour units range from 5 to 50 tonnes and many forms now exist, including cubes, tetrapods, dolosse, tribars, stabits and cobs.

As high loadings can be imposed on the foreshore using armour units, a check should be made on the stability of the

184

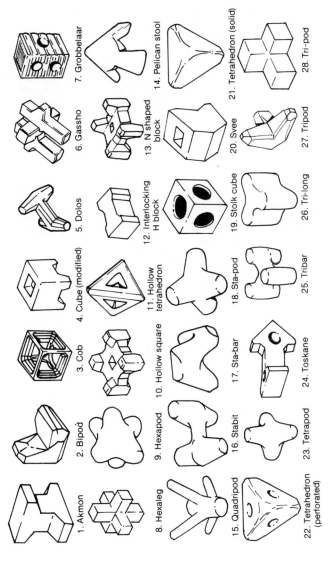

1. Akmon 2. Bipod 3. Cob 4. Cube (modified) 5. Dolos 6. Gassho 7. Grobbelaar
8. Hexaleg 9. Hexapod 10. Hollow square 11. Hollow tetrahedron 12. Interlocking H block 13. N shaped block 14. Pelican stool
15. Quadripod 16. Stabit 17. Sta-bar 18. Sta-pod 19. Stolk cube 20. Svee 21. Tetrahedron (solid)
22. Tetrahedron (perforated) 23. Tetrapod 24. Toskane 25. Tribar 26. Tri-long 27. Tripod 28. Tri-pod

Fig. 71.   Armour units (illustration reproduced by permission of the Controller, HMSO, courtesy of Hydraulics Research Station, Wallingford)

185

foreshore against a rotational or wedge failure. Similarly the design must ensure that at the point at which the armour units join the foreshore increased erosion does not occur causing a toe failure. Wave turbulence in the interstices of the units may cause material to be carried seawards in suspension, particularly sand-sized particles and fines. This in turn could result in settlement of the units at the base of the structure and hence reduced efficiency in absorbing wave attack but can be prevented by the use of filters, (Section 3.4). Fig. 71 shows examples of the units. Tetrapods weighing about 4 Mg each were used in the strengthening of the Marine Drive sea wall at Bombay, India.

6.6 FRIABLE CLIFF STABILISATION

Works to prevent erosion of friable cliffs such as chalk and sandstone are frequently required. Generally, they will stand at a nearly vertical slope for a considerable period of time, but both are readily eroded by the action of wind, water and frost.

The general procedure is to

(*a*) stabilise and accrete the foreshore by one of the methods described in this book

(*b*) provide, if necessary, a longitudinal wall to protect the toe of the cliff; this may be permeable or impermeable and take the form of one of the types of wall described in this book

(*c*) grade back the cliff to a stable slope.

Fig. 72. Graded chalk cliffs with toe protection works

When protected by soil and vegetation the sandstone is usually stable in nature at a slope of about 40°. In practice it is difficult to stabilise slopes greater than about 35° owing to the problems of rapidly establishing and maintaining a cover of soil.

Fig. 72 shows graded chalk cliffs at Westgate, Kent, combined with (toe) protective and amenity works. The cliffs are graded to a minimum angle of 15° to the vertical to minimise the risk of falls caused by frost action and to keep the line of the protective works at the toe of the cliffs as uniform as practicable.

6.7 SOIL MECHANICS OF CLAY CLIFF STABILISATION

Along the coastline of this country large lengths of clay cliffs exist. They present special problems when the designer is considering the form of protection required. Any instability of the slope may cause failure of the toe protection.

In their natural state clays will stand at slopes of 10 : 1 to 20 : 1. Any steeper slope which has not been protected will usually be subject to movement. This movement can take the form of large deep-seated slips, shallow surface movements or the movement of one zone of clay over another. The movements can be circular or non-circular in shape.

Before the designer can interpret the form of failure on the site in question a site investigation, soil tests and the installation of instrumentation should be carried out. When considering the type of instrumentation required the designer has the choice of purpose-developed equipment, which can be used to monitor slopes (see also Section 3.7).

Movement of the slope can be measured by the use of inclinometers. This equipment consists of two main components. The first is an aluminium or glass fibre tube which is inserted and grouted within the clay slope using a bentonite grout. As the slope moves it deforms the tube. This deformation is measured by inserting an instrument down the tube to obtain an angular difference or a displacement in millimetres. The readings are compared with an original or base reading and the true movement obtained. Fig. 73 shows such equipment.

Second, pore pressures within the soil can be obtained by the installation and reading of piezometers. These are usually of

187

Fig. 73.   Inclinometer equipment

three types, the first being the porous pot dip meter type. This consists of a porous tip linked to a polythene tube 25 mm in diameter. The water level is determined by the insertion of a probe which is connected to a warning light, bell or buzzer via a calibrated cable, this warning device being set off by the contact of the probe with the water surface. This type of instrument has the advantages of ease of installation, low cost and simplicity of use. It is, however, slow to settle to a true value which may limit its use.

The second type of instrument is the pneumatic type. This consists of a special tip which is linked to the reading point via twin plastic tubes. The instrument is read with a calibrated unit which contains the nitrogen gas reservoir, this gas being chosen for its inert qualities. Again operation is simple. The

188

instrument has great advantages over the first type in that readings can be obtained within two to three weeks of installation. It has the disadvantage of being more expensive to install and needs more complex reading equipment which, although reliable, needs to be kept in peak condition to ensure accurate results.

The third type is the twin line hydraulic piezometer which has a principle of operation similar to that of the pneumatic instrument except that the gas is replaced by water as the operating agent. The instrument tip is again connected to the reading point via twin plastic lines. Readings may be obtained using similar equipment to the pneumatic instrument or by the termination of the instrument with others in a reading house. The instruments can then be read via a manifold or via a manometer mounted on the wall of the house. As water is used care must be taken to ensure that the instrument is not affected by adverse weather. This form of instrument is arguably the most reliable of the instruments discussed, giving rapid accurate readings after installation. It can be maintained after installation and may be used to determine in situ permeability. Its susceptibility to weather and the need to provide group reading points limit its use.

Finally, if the designer wishes only to know if movement has occurred, a slip indicator may be used. This is a simple instrument consisting of a polythene tube bentonite grouted into the site, a metal rod 900 mm long lowered to the bottom of the tube via a wire, and left at that position. If subsequently the rod can be easily drawn to the top no movement has occurred. As soon as the rod becomes difficult to draw up this is an indication of movement. The instrument is simple and cheap to install. However, it lacks the sophistication of the inclinometer system and cannot quantify the amount of movement.

Much work has been carried out on the theoretical behaviour of slopes. Most analytical methods divide the possible or actual slipped zone into slices to evaluate the forces, both disturbing and resisting, as a sum of the slice contributions. The limit equilibrium method evaluates the overall stability of the sliding mass using some or all of the three equations of static equilibrium of plane problem. Morgenstern and Price set out a method of analysis which allows calculations to be carried out without the need to place restriction upon the shape of the possible slip surface.[2,3]

When treating movements in clay it is usual to carry out grading works removing the worst of the forces causing imbalance. It is also usual to carry out works to reduce the pore pressure within the clay, causing increases in the clay strength. Such reductions in pore pressure may, in some cases, take many years to attain and, as a result, the problems of movement can remain for many years after treatment.

Chapter 3 gives the designer simple analytical methods which are applicable to clay slope stability problems. But problems of coast protection regarding clay slope stability often require methods of analysis using computer programs.

In London clays the minimum strength usually occurs with soil parameters of $C = 0$ and $\phi = 20°$. The designer should note there is a reduction in strength with the passage of time, ϕ normally remaining constant. At Herne Bay it was considered that broadly the clay would have parameters of $C = 14$ KN/m^2 initially, reducing to 2.3 KN/m^2 after 50 years and zero after 100 years of life. Works are therefore usually designed for a given duration, i.e. a given design life. (For further information on residual strength see reference 7 and reference 23, Chapter 4.)

The advent of specific programs for both circular and non-circular slips are exemplified by Slip Circle 1 and Non-Circular Slip 1 of Genesys Limited, of Loughborough, which are based upon the Morgenstern and Price theory previously mentioned. This allows the designer access to methods allowing for many variables. The use of such programs is recommended as their availability allows speedy investigations of many cases of potential failure within the clay slope at low cost. Equally however, the advent of computer calculated factors of safety should not influence the designer unduly. Any factor of safety against failure of a clay slope having a value between unity and 1.2 should be considered as critical and such a slope is worthy of treatment using any of the following methods.

6.8 GRADING AND SURFACE DRAINAGE

If the movement has been analysed as suggested in the previous Section and the problem has been found to include

Fig. 74. Herringbone drainage system

191

shallow surface movements, it is suggested that the slope be treated by means of surface grading associated with the installation of a herringbone collection drainage system.

Fig. 74 shows a coastal clay slope at Herne Bay which has been treated by this means. The slopes range from 3 : 1 to 10 : 1. Fig. 75 (a) and (b) shows the typical construction of the types of drain installed within the slope. The depth of the slip will govern the depth of drain to be installed as well as the spacings of the system. Reference to Fig. 75 (c) provides the designer with guidance for the depth against spacing of drains in clay soils.

Generally such treatment will give adequate factors of safety for the works within their design life. Attention should be drawn, however, to the fact that the weathering process of clays will lead to reduced factors of safety with the passage of time.

Planting shrubs and vegetation should be encouraged as such works have a beneficial effect on long-term slope stability and have the additional advantages of low cost and providing an improved appearance.

6.9 SPIDER DRAINS

Consideration can now be given as to the treatment of deep movements in clay. Stability can be improved by carrying out one or more of the following methods of stabilisation:

(*a*) regrading

(*b*) toe-weighting

(*c*) reducing the pore pressures on the slip plane.

In some cases regrading may be inappropriate because of its effect upon the upper slopes above the slip.

Toe weighting is an effective means of treatment, but to obtain appreciable increases in the factor of safety a large salient often needs to be constructed. Such a salient would normally be on the seaward side of the sea defences and would form an obstruction against the littoral transfer process in addition to undesirable lee erosion.

The method of reduction of pore pressures at the slip plane requires careful calculation of the possible improved factor of safety. The pore pressure change on the slip plane in relation to time can be calculated using the two dimensional finite dif-

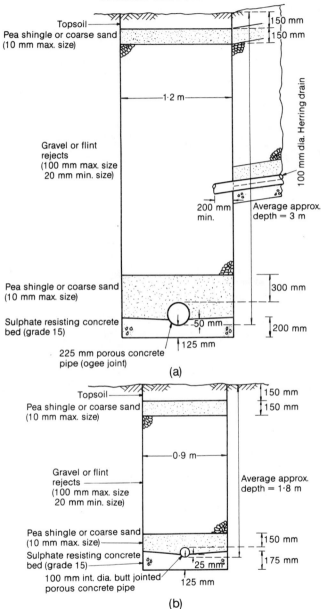

Fig. 75. *Section through (a) herringbone drain; (b) primary drain;*
(c) see p. 194

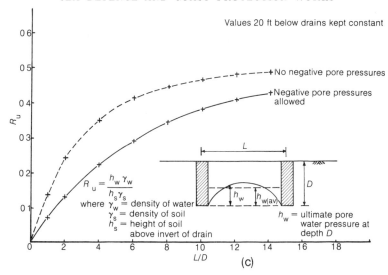

Fig. 75 (c).   Depth against spacing of drains in clay soils

ference method based upon Terzaghi's Consolidation Theory
(reference 11, Chapter 3). The pore pressure change so calculated is then utilised in the slope stability method devised by
Bishop.[4]

One possible method of reducing pore pressures across the
slip plane if a permeable stratum exists underneath the clay
slope is the installation of vertical drainage. This is set out in
Section 6.10.

Consideration can also be given to the installation of a drainage system within the slipped mass. One possible method for
such works is the provision of vertical large diameter shafts
acting as collection sumps for a system of horizontal bored
drains drilled radially from the shafts at set levels.

Such a choice was made in the stabilisation works carried
out by Canterbury City Council at East Cliff, Herne Bay. The
movement was saucer-shaped having a diameter of 125 m and
a maximum depth of 14 m. The remedial works consisted of the
construction of four reinforced concrete shafts 14 m deep and
4 m internal diameter. From these shafts 100 mm diameter
drains were drilled radially into the clay by means of full flight
augers. Porous land drains of 100 mm diameter were inserted
into the holes so bored, the clay being strong enough to support

194

the circular hole. A total of 2500 m of drains were installed in this manner.

The shafts were linked together and a pump inserted in the lowest collector shaft. Ground water was pumped out through a rising main and flow meter to an outfall and discharged into the sea.

Since the installation of the system of drainage in the slip an average of 160 litres of ground water per week has been pumped out.

Great care was taken during construction to ensure that an adequate distance was allowed between the underlying sandstone and the base of the lowest shaft to prevent the failure of the layer of clay by heaving upwards through the excavation.

Prior to the installation of the drains, movements of 13 mm per year had been recorded in the sea walls These were reduced to 6 mm in the first year after the completion of the works. Since that date no further movement has been recorded. It was calculated that a 30% increase in the factor of safety has probably been obtained with the installation of spider drains.

6.10 VERTICALLY INSTALLED DRAINS

Where the slope is underlain by a permeable stratum, consideration can be given to the provision of vertically installed drains linking the clay to the permeable stratum underneath. Care must be taken to check that an adequate reduction in pore pressure will occur upon the installation of vertical drainage. In certain circumstances reverse flow could occur through the drains increasing pore pressures instead of reducing them.

In treating a site with vertical drains it is advantageous to place drain centres closely to ensure their maximum effect. To date little has been done in this country using vertical drainage as a means of stabilisation. The main application has been in embankment construction to dissipate excess pore pressure and to minimise settlement.

Resulting from this, little information is available upon the types of drain and their suitability of use in clay slopes. The various types of drains available are reviewed by Hansbo.[5]

Considerable success has been achieved by Cementation Ground Engineering using their sand-filled polyester sock

195

drain. This is installed by vertical rotary drills, the drain being lowered into the hole so formed. Other types of drain take the form of the wick system. Most of these drains are based on the Kjellman cardboard wick, which was a band shaped drain 3.5 mm by 100 mm made up of two cardboard strips with ten longitudinal grooves glued together in such a way that the grooves form longitudinal channels. This drain was first used in 1937. Today most systems have a core of plastic material with a filter sleeve of paper, or more commonly, a plastic filter fabric.

The installation of the wick type drains can be by either pre-drilling or by the dynamic insertion of mandril to which the drain is attached. Care should be taken that such a system can be inserted through the clay taking into account obstructions such as clay stones. As the efficiency of the drain as a whole relies upon its ability to direct flow into the permeable stratum it must go some considerable distance into that stratum. To date this problem has limited the use of wick system drains despite their economic advantages and speed of installation.

Finally, one untried system shows promise. This combines the circular shaped sock of a sand drain with a grooved porous plastic land drain. To date this system has not been tried in this country.

REFERENCES

1 YOUNG R. M., ACKERS P. and THOMPSON D. M. *Riprap Design for Wind-wave Attack; Prototype Tests on the Offshore Bank in the Wash*. Technical note no. 84. London, Construction Industry Research and Information Association, 1977.

2 MORGENSTERN N. R. and PRICE V. E. The analysis of the stability of general slip surfaces. *Géotechnique*, 1965, **15,** No. 1, 79.

3 MORGENSTERN N. R. and PRICE V. E. A numerical method of solving the equations of stability of general slip surfaces. *Computer J.*, 1967, **9,** No. 4, 338–393.

4 BISHOP A. W. The use of slip circle in the stability analysis of slopes. *Géotechnique*, 1955, **5,** No. 1, 7–17.

5   HANSBO S. Consolidation of clay by band-shaped prefabri-
cated drains. *Ground Engng*, 1979, **12,** No. 5.

6   SKEMPTON A. W. Long term stability of clay slopes. *Géotechnique*, 1964, **14,** No. 2, 77–102.

Chapter 7

Closure of breaches in sea walls

7.1 BREACHES

The most difficult breaches to deal with, in sea walls, are those in walls protecting low-lying land. While breaches similar in all respects seldom occur, there are general principles of closure that apply to the successful closing of all breaches. Careful planning is of the highest importance—ill-considered expedients will seldom succeed.

A clear picture must first be formed of the site circumstances and details of the breach and of the labour, plant and materials available. Logical application of the basic principles of breach closure will then provide the correct solution to the problem.

Breaches often occur in very inaccessible places and the construction of a suitable access then becomes a major part of the emergency works.

7.2 CAUSES OF BREACHES

The main causes of sea wall failure are set out in Section 3.1. Breaches usually result from direct frontal erosion by wave action, flow through the fissured zone, scour of the landward face by over-topping, or combinations of these causes.

7.3 PRINCIPLES OF BREACH CLOSURE

The first aims must be to limit as far as possible further erosion of the breach and to reduce the volume and the velocity of the water flowing through it (see Figs. 76–78).

A clear distinction must be made between (*a*) breaches through which the water flows only at high tide and (*b*) those where the water flows continously, either in or out according to

Fig. 76.   Breach at high tide

Fig. 77.   Breach at low tide; ring wall under construction

199

Fig. 78.   Completed ring wall round breach

the state of the tide.

In the case of (*a*) it is usual to fill the breach with clay-filled sandbags (Fig. 79). At a later date, when site conditions are suitable and plant, labour and materials are available, the bag-work can be removed and the wall can then be permanently reinstated. Sometimes it is possible to construct a ring wall of sandbags, or of pickets and sheeting, or of trench sheeting backed by sandbags, or of similar materials, on the seaward side of the breach, to keep out the tide. This is the procedure usually adopted when it is expected that permanent recon-struction can be carried out fairly soon.

A condition intermediate between (*a*) and (*b*) can occur when, although water only enters the breach from the sea near the top of the tide, nevertheless because the marshes are fairly deeply flooded, water flows out through the breach as the tide drops. The ring wall should then be built on the marsh on the landward side of the breach.

Efforts must also be made to get rid of the water on the marshes, as soon as possible, through existing gravity outfalls,

Fig. 79.   Closure of breach by clay-filled sand-bags

if they are of adequate capacity (see Section 3.17) or through controlled breaches in the sea walls. Controlled breaches can be used with deep flooding when, as usually happens, the damage occurs at a time of exceptionally high tide and the lower tides following do not reach the level of the water in the marshes.

Breaches of type (*b*) present far greater difficulties. The first step is to stop the breach widening by providing, if needed, protection at the sides of the breach. The next step is to build a ring wall, usually on uneroded marshland on the landward side of the breach. Even while under construction, this reduces the inflow and outflow of water which becomes less and less as the ring wall is built up until, when the top of the ring wall is above tide level (or the level of the water on the marshes, whichever is the highest), flow through the breach finally ceases. The Schelphoek breach in the Island of Schouwen in Holland, one of the biggest breaches ever to be closed, was closed by constructing a landward ring wall of caissons sunk on to a prepared bed of willow mattresses that prevented erosion under

201

the caissons. For large and difficult breaches of this kind it is customary to carry out model investigations to ensure the success of the operations.

7.4 BREACHES IN SEA WALL REVETMENTS

Breaches in sea wall revetments are generally less difficult to deal with than breaches that let water through.

Similar principles apply to emergency works for damaged facings as for wall breaches. Every effort must be made to prevent the damage spreading by providing protection at the perimeter of the damaged area. This is often in the form of concrete drop walls constructed with rapid-hardening cement or with a quick-setting additive to the cement. The bed of the damaged area can be covered with concrete of the same mix. Fabric mattresses filled with cement/sand grout by pumping can also be used for emergency protection. Once repairs of this kind have been made, the permanent reinstatement works can be carried out when site conditions are more favourable and plant, labour and materials more readily available.

Appendix

Design charts

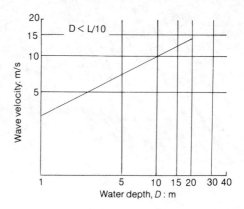

Design Chart A.   Wave velocities in 'shallow' water for various depths

*Design Chart B. (Overleaf.)   Deep water (SMB) wave heights and
periods and limiting wind durations for various fetches and wind speeds*

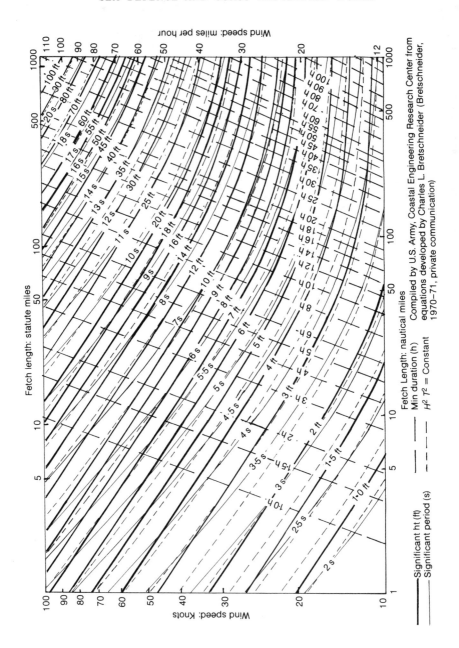

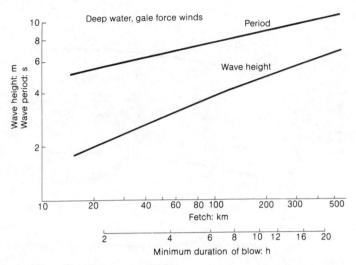

Design Chart C.   Deep water (SMB) wave heights and periods and minimum durations of blow for gale force winds

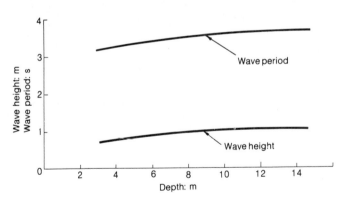

Design Chart D.   Shallow water (SPM) wave heights and periods with gale force winds; fetch: 5 km

205

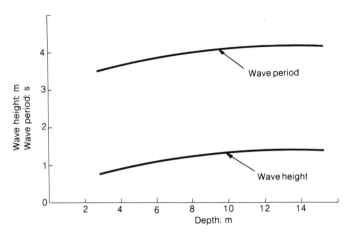

Design Chart E.   Shallow water (SPM) wave heights and periods with gale force winds; fetch: 10 km

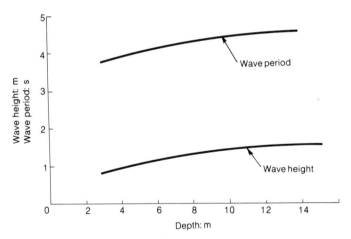

Design Chart F.   Shallow water (SPM) wave heights and periods with gale force winds; fetch: 15 km

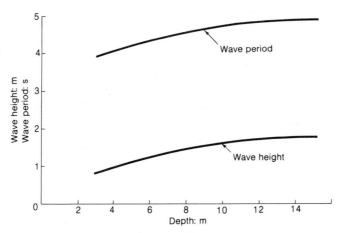

Design Chart G.   Shallow water (SPM) wave heights and periods with gale force winds; fetch: 20 km

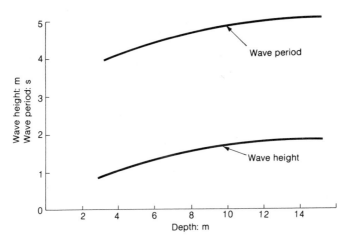

Design Chart H.   Shallow water (SPM) wave heights and periods with gale force winds; fetch: 25 km

207

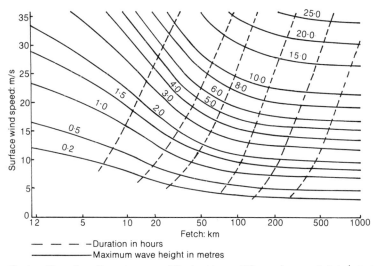

Design Chart I.   Oceanic waters (Derbyshire and Draper); wave height/wind speed/duration/fetch relationships

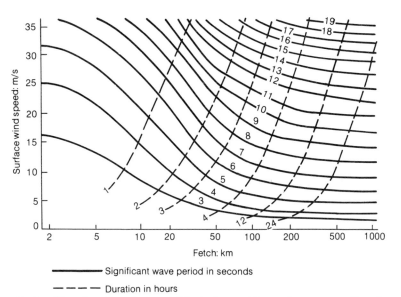

Design Chart J.   Oceanic waters (Derbyshire and Draper); wave period/wind speed/duration/fetch relationships

208

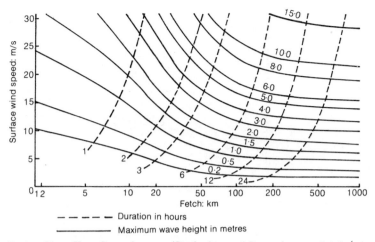

Design Chart K.   Coastal waters (Derbyshire and Draper); wave height/
wind speed/duration/fetch relationships

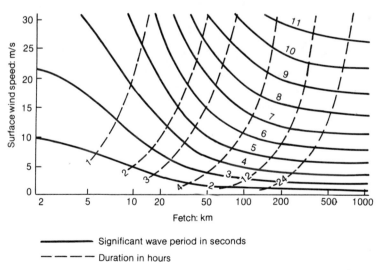

Design Chart L.   Coastal waters (Derbyshire and Draper); wave period/
wind speed/duration/fetch relationships

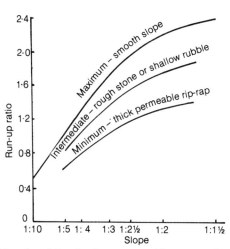

Design Chart M.   Swash heights for various uniform apron slopes for smooth, intermediate rough stones or shallow riprap and thick permeable riprap (reproduced with permission from ICE Report on 'Floods and reservoir safety')

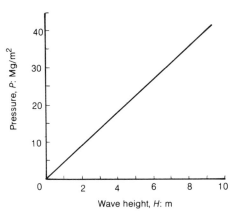

Design Chart N.   Wave pressures corresponding to various wave heights (in Mg/m². Multiply by 9.81 to convert to kN)

210

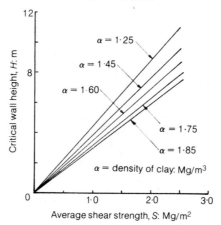

Design Chart O.   Critical wall heights corresponding to various clay densities and shear strengths (in Mg/m². Multiply by 9.81 to convert to kN)

211

Index